Acupuncture Principles
and
Your Health

Acupuncture Principles
and
Your Health

James B. Howland, C.A.

AURICLE PRESS
499 Humboldt Street
Santa Rosa, CA 95404

Acupuncture Principles
and
Your Health

Published by: Auricle Press
499 Humboldt Street
Santa Rosa, California 95404, USA

First Edition   September 1981
Second Printing   December 1981

Copyright © 1981 by James B. Howland
Cover drawing and illustrations copyright © 1981 by Kim C. Howland
Library of Congress Catalogue Card #81-68882
Printed in the United States of America
ISBN 0-939904-00-4

Dedication

This book is dedicated to Master George Long who taught me the Science of Acupuncture and the Art of Learning.

Table of Contents

Foreword

"Holistic Health"

We hear and read about this increasingly popular concept more and more. Yet what does it really mean? And, how does one achieve it?

The concept is actually not a new one. We in the West are simply rediscovering for ourselves an approach that the East has understood and practiced for millenia. What they have known and what we are just beginning to explore is that any truly effective approach to healing must focus not on "sick" body parts, but the whole person. And, by "whole person" is meant mind and body, and more. Spirit, intellect, emotions, belief systems, family ties, work, community, indeed the whole physical and social environment are all relevant. Systems within systems within systems.

Nowhere is this holistic understanding of the East better articulated than in the practice of acupuncture. By now, most Americans probably associate acupuncture with its use as an analgesic for painless surgery. Most of us have seen television films of some patient in China gaily chatting while surgeons poke about in a gaping chest cavity. We tend to think of acupuncture as a very focused, technical treatment, perhaps something akin to flipping on or off tiny electrical switches with fine needles. Yet more important than the complex technical details of the needle-work itself is the philosophic overview which guides it.

It is not so much the needles which heal as it is the skilled practitioner who is able to elicit the forces of self-healing which lie dormant in his patient. The needles are but one tool among many which are even more subtle through which the acupuncturist sensitizes his patient to the healing forces within. This practitioner is himself one who understands and practices balanced living and the harmony of mind and body. Such a practitioner is James Howland, the author of the slim volume you hold in your hands.

Other books on acupuncture have tended to suffer from being too technical or theoretical for the interested layperson. Or they have run to the other extreme of being excessively simplified overviews by journalists who lacked the depth and authority of first- hand knowledge. Another problem, of course, has been that most of the really authoritative books on the subject have been written by Oriental practitioners. Such books are plagued by all the inherent weaknesses of translation, not to mention the seeming "strangeness" of Eastern thought.

Now, at last, we have a really practical and useful book written from the perspective of a Westerner who has a deep understanding of what he is writing about, rooted in his own experience.

Seven years ago, James Howland began an apprenticeship with Master George Long, one of San Francisco's foremost Chinese acupuncturists. In other words, he learned acupuncture in the traditional way, through doing, gaining first-hand practical knowledge from closely supervised work with thousands of patients that no amount of book study could have achieved. The master-apprentice relationship included not only the study of acupuncture technique, but also the system of Chinese philosophy and psychology of which acupuncture is but a part. Already a long time student of the martial arts, Howland has also been instructed in Tai Chi Chuan, both as a moving meditation and as a form of self-defense. Out of this rich mixture of direct experience and Howland's predilection for wideranging academic studies comes this synthesis which is unique, personal and practical. More than anything else, Howland has sought to become a "man of knowledge," and the degree to which he has achieved this high goal sets this volume above any mere translation of Oriental ideas.

This book will prove useful not only to those interested in acupuncture, but to all who are interested in leading whole and balanced lives.

David Van Nuys, Ph. D.
Professor of Psychology
Sonoma State University

Acknowledgements

My deep and heartfelt appreciation to my immediate family:

Kim, for her love, assistance and understanding during a difficult time; Jamen and Shandon, for coming to this world and giving me the opportunity to love and grow with them; And to my Dad and Margie, Jim and Mary Bryant, and Fred Steele, special thanks.

I would also like to acknowledge various and sundry contributions (too numerous to detail) as follows:

L. Avilla, Marc Berger, John Cole C.A. and Family, Lum Ding, Dr. Luther Distler and Family, Ron Dong C.A. and Family, Mark Fishkin, Dr. David G. Fraser and Family, Dr. Suzanne Graham, Tom Lennon, Rose Murray, Suzanne Robinson, Dr. David Van Nuys, and Joan, Dana and Zia Ziprin.

In regard to the production of this book, thank you, thank you, thank you to:

Stephanie Mines, Super Secretary and C. W. "Bill" and Charlotte Meisterfeld (MRK Publishing).

If there is anyone who has helped me along the way who has not been mentioned, this is for you:

THANK YOU

Personal Background

Personal Background

I did not set out to become an acupuncturist. My first contact with acupuncture was through the martial arts. My interest and involvement with the martial arts goes back over twenty years when I studied judo in order to strengthen my body after an auto accident. I had been told I would be a partial cripple the rest of my life but was not willing to accept that condition. I decided to see what I could do myself using mind and body to restore my health. I went to college at age 18, and immediately signed up for swimming, which I had not previously learned. I also began studying judo as a way to strengthen my "bad leg." After becoming involved in judo, I discovered that not only was I able to get back to a so- called normal state, but I was able to do many things supposedly normal people could not do; that my "bad leg" was better than most people's good legs. I learned that very little is known about the potential of the human mind and body when directed by an act of will. This began a life-long involvement with the martial arts in one form or another, and through the martial arts, the healing arts.

Many times people ask me what the relationship is between the martial arts and the healing arts. Sometimes, for dramatic effect, I explain that it means that I can either set a broken arm or break one. But it is true that the training for the martial arts and the healing arts overlaps. They are both examples of practical applications of the principles of Yin and Yang. Understanding these two forces means that their energy can be applied in many ways. It's not that Yang is good and Yin is bad, or vice-versa. They're two forces that mutually interpenetrate and create each other. The martial arts are systematic ways of understanding these forces and energies and working with them in a physiological and psychological way. The healing arts are also techniques and ways to understand those energies and work with them to bring about a natural state, a state of balance and harmony.

I went to Master George Long to learn White Crane Gung Fu because I had studied many different forms of martial arts and I had heard he was one of the best martial arts teachers in the Bay Area. After starting Gung Fu with him, I began to see the amazing changes in the people who went into and came out of his treatment room, adjacent to his Gung Fu studio. After I had been studying with him for a while, I was going back to Arizona to open a Tai Chi Chuan studio. Before I left, he asked me if I would be interested in studying acupuncture. I said, "No, I want to go back and teach Tai Chi Chuan." I did go back to Arizona but while I was there I talked on the phone to Ron Dong, Master Long's chief assistant. He indicated there was a great deal of activity in the clinic and that was a good time to learn acupuncture, when lots of people were coming for treatment. I reconsidered and closed down the Tai Chi Chuan studio that I had opened and went back to the Bay Area to study acupuncture.

I wondered why Master Long had picked me as an apprentice because I hadn't been looking to learn acupuncture. I had seen people come in and ask him to teach them and I had seen him turn them down. I figured he must have seen something in me to indicate I had the potential to learn the skills he was teaching combined with an ability to communicate with people. Studying as a traditional apprentice, I worked eight hours a day, five and a half days a week at the clinic. I put in over a thousand hours seeing 30-40 people a day. When I began treating people on my own, I did it on my day off, driving from the Bay Area to Santa Rosa. So a great deal of experience was packed into a fairly short amount of time.

My apprenticeship was unlike Western education, and for that reason few Westerners have really been trained in the martial and healing arts. It's not classrooms and memorization and reading and studying. It's practical experience and learning things with your body as well as your mind and understanding things directly. In the past seven years, I have done quite a bit of public speaking, which I enjoy. I like answering people's questions and talking *with* them, having a dialogue, a dialectic, finding out what they are interested in. One of the healthier aspects of my profession is that I was trained to know what I know and to know what I don't know. When I don't know something, I make efforts to learn it. When you are willing to admit you don't know something it makes life a lot easier. Sometimes I describe my apprenticeship as being around a Fritz Perls who could kick and punch because it was directly involved with the martial arts as a practical, day-to-day way of encountering life. You had to be able to apply things with your body. That's why we learned breathing techniques and physical exercises, because it's not enough to have knowledge in your head, you have to be able to use it and apply it. For that reason, we were not allowed to take notes in the treatment room. We did not read books because Master Long said books would just confuse us and taking notes was of no use because what happens if there's an emergency and you don't have your notebook? What kind of doctor are you? The idea was to obtain practical skills, things that you took with you and were able to apply on the spot.

The first thing I learned from Master Long was how to treat headaches. And when I had thoroughly learned how to treat headaches, I learned to treat something else. I've learned to treat one problem at a time. Similarly, I learned Chinese pulse diagnosis by my teacher saying, "Here, feel this. This is a good kidney pulse. Here, feel this. This is a bad liver pulse." I also learned one pulse at a time.

Instead of talking to people in parables, Master Long talked about their cars. I thought this strange at first, but then began to see it was very appropriate. People knew more about their cars than they knew about their bodies. If you asked somebody where their spleen or pancreas was, they didn't know. But if you said, "Well, it's like your carburetor" they'd say, "Oh, yeah, my carburetor. I understand that." So people would come in for overhauls and tune-ups.

I've given more than 10,000 treatments. I've treated everything from hemorrhoids to headaches, helped deliver babies, and I've treated a number of so-called "incurables" with acupuncture. And, after seven years of private practice, every day I'm amazed at the human mind-body complex and its potential to heal itself.

Acupuncture and Traditional Oriental Medicine

Acupuncture and Traditional Oriental Medicine

Introduction and Overview

One of the major premises of Oriental medicine is that of Yin and Yang. They are represented in the Tai Chi diagram by a circle with intertwining elements of black and white, each with a dot of the other in its center. The diagram represents the flow of energy in the universe and the constant interchange between Yin and Yang. Yin and Yang are dark and light, night and day, cold and hot, sweet and sour, left and right, down and up. They are polarities. They're different from the Western concept of opposing polarities because the Chinese say that each creates the other. Instead of a linear representation, it's circular or cyclic, where one, when it goes to the extreme, turns into the other. Instead of saying there is good and evil, and that good must triumph and wipe out evil, or that evil is trying to destroy good, the Chinese say they mutually create each other. They turn into each other, and the idea is to understand the flow, the change from one to the other, rather than hold onto one and avoid the other.

A good example of this is in breathing. We inhale and we exhale. We don't say, "Gee, I really like to inhale, but I hate to let go of anything, so I think I'm just going to inhale for the next three or four days." Well, we can't do it. It may sound ridiculous in relation to breathing, but we often do that in many areas of our lives. What gives us our vitality or Chi (the Chinese word for life force) is the process of breathing. We inhale; we exhale. And this interplay gives us life or vitality. We can't do all of one or the other. There has to be balance between them.

The Chinese say to understand the Tai Chi diagram and the interplay of Yin and Yang, you must understand not only a metaphysical system, but you must know how to *apply* it in your life. The principle of balance comes out in Tai Chi Chuan. Chuan means "fist" and Tai Chi, as in the diagram, means "Supreme Ultimate." So Tai Chi Chuan means "Supreme Ultimate Fist," or "Supreme Ultimate Boxing." In the physical form of Tai Chi Chuan there is an advanced practice called pushing hands, which is another way of applying the principles of Yin and Yang and their interplay.

The Chinese talk about and look for balance and harmony between forces, and in pushing hands, you move in a circular pattern in relation to your opponent's movements. If you become too linear in an aggressive fashion, pushing too much, you will pull yourself off balance. On the other hand, if you yield too much, you will pull yourself off your own center and allow yourself to be overturned by your opponent.

If you move in a circle you become sensitive to those points and wonder, "Am I pushing too hard?" "Am I getting away from my own center?" Or, "Am I yielding too much?" "Am I losing my integrity by yielding?" The idea is if you move in a circle, you balance the two forces. And the practice is, if you do not acknowledge and use and recognize those two forces and the balance between them, you will become uprooted, and it will look like your opponent uprooted you, but actually it will be your own lack of self-balance which has uprooted you.

Acupuncture and Traditional Oriental Medicine

The concepts of Yin and Yang, balance, harmony, Tai Chi, circles, cycles, rhythm — these things will be mentioned time and time again in the process of what I'm saying.

These forces apply in all Chinese arts because essentially there's only one art, the art of living. If you have a system which is really good, really solid, it will apply in more areas than one. That's always the test of it. Philosophy is to see, "Does it apply intellectually or is it something I can use in my life? Does it apply to other fields?" In driving a car, there is over-steer and under-steer, too much or not enough, and you have a problem. Racing drivers talk about the line they follow through a particular corner. There is a path, a way to take their vehicles through that corner at the edge of its capabilities. The edge of capability will vary with different vehicles, whether it's a Grand Prix, Formula 1, sports car or whatever category of car. The capability of the car will be different but the line for that particular kind of car will be specific in relation to the factors involved. A different driver may be able to go closer to the "ideal" line, but the basic way of balancing the forces through the corner will remain the same.

In the martial arts, Yin and Yang become when to be aggressive and attack and when to be passive and yield. In the healing arts, this translates into balancing the energy of the body with an understanding that the body is one thing, one whole. Western culture has become more and more specialized. But the Oriental perspective is that the body is a whole and you cannot affect one part of it without affecting all of it.

Yin is not enough energy and Yang is too much energy. Techniques like acupuncture, acupressure and herbs, massage and exercise are designed to help balance the body's energy and stimulate the body to heal itself. Another premise of Oriental medicine is that no one else heals you or your body. The body is reminded of its own wisdom and repairs itself.

When the body is separated into parts, it doesn't work. The body is like a family and all its parts are related. For example, if you damage your liver, you will also inadvertently damage your kidneys. When the liver can't do its job, it borrows energy from the kidneys, so the kidneys may suffer from something done to the liver. In Western terms this may not make sense, but it makes physiological sense and so you have to understand that all of your organs are like a family. If something happens to one, it affects the others.

An obvious example is that if you step on a rusty nail, you can't say, "Well, it's a tiny little hole in my foot; it's not going to affect anything else. I'll just ignore it." Through the system of circulation in the body, the rusty nail can cause blood poisoning which will quickly kill the whole organism. You have to take into account the effect on the whole being. The Chinese carry it one step further and say it's not just the body. There are no psychiatrists in China because they consider the mind and body to be one. We have both. So far no patient has come into my office and left his or her mind at home. And no one has sent their mind in and left their body at home. We have both. We need to work with both.

A person came to me who had been with a medical team visiting China and they were shown healing facilities and therapeutic methods. The psychiatrists in the group were upset. They thought the Chinese were hiding something because they never met any psychiatrists. They had a hard time accepting that they didn't use psychiatrists in China because they dealt with people's mental and emotional problems *along with* their physiological problems.

One of the fascinating parts of my job as I see it is to blend East and West. I am Caucasian, brought up in Western culture, yet the Eastern methods, techniques and ways of perceiving and doing things often seem more natural to me than the things I learned here. So what I look for is a blend of the best from East

24

and West, whatever is appropriate in the combination that works, just as we have two hemispheres of the brain. We don't want to operate only through the logical, rational, linear side all the time, nor can we always operate from the emotional, holistic, intuitive, musical side. We need both sides; we need both aspects. We can't be totally run by our emotions; we can't be totally run by our logic. We have to use our consciousness to choose what is appropriate in each situation.

Many people feel that in the East the tendency to go within results in withdrawal from reality. They point to the fact that in many places in the East people are starving because of a culture focused too much on the inner without attending to the outer. In the West, on the other hand, the focus is on outward expansion, controlling and manipulating nature, with very little emphasis on the inner world. What's important is a balance between the two. It's not all inner or outer. It's just that each makes the other more effective. The more you go in, the more you learn respect, awe and wonder. The more you come out and apply that, the more balanced your life is. This balance between East and West is apparent in current medical training in China. I have been told the training is three years of traditional medicine (acupuncture, herbs, therapeutic exercise — another name for Gung Fu, breathing techniques) and three years of Western medicine (antibiotics, injections and surgery). One is not totally better than the other but, instead, each has something to offer of what's necessary for current circumstances.

A Chinese doctor would choose to apply whatever is appropriate. As China becomes more industrialized there are more industrial accidents so they have developed Western surgical reconstructive techniques in order to deal with the realities of the situation. However, in small communities and in communes throughout China, the barefoot doctor provides primary health care because 85% of people's problems can be treated on a local level safely and effectively. The hospitals are not burdened with routine cases and can become specialized treatment centers rather than catch-alls.

Change

Another one of those premises that's so important is "the only thing that never changes is the fact that everything changes." If we don't acknowledge that, we create problems for ourselves. We get out of sync with the cycles in our lives and create mental, physical and emotional imbalances. The job of any health practitioner should be to help people get back in touch with their natural cycles.

Harmony

The key to all Oriental arts whether the martial arts or the healing arts, the fine arts, archery, flower arranging, painting or calligraphy, is harmony. It means harmony in our families, harmony in our relationships with others and in our bodies, and harmony in our relationship with our environment. I was reading a book where there was an Earth Day Celebration and a scientist came to give a talk about cleaning up the air. He was a fairly well known person whose name I won't mention. He was to talk on the environment and how important it was to clean up the air, and he was smoking! There's a certain inconsistency there with him polluting his own internal environment while wanting to clean up the external environment. It's important to find the kind of balance we need without being mechanical about applying the principles of balance in our lives. An interesting factor about these principles is that if you start thinking about balance, about harmonizing things, you can do it in almost any process. You can do it in how you approach tasks around the house. For example, I used to hate doing dishes. My way to deal with things that I hate is to do them, and do them and do them and do them. I forced myself to do dishes over and over until I found I liked dishes. I made dishwashing a form of meditation. It had to be done. You can't just say, "Well, I really ate that meal well, I cleaned those dishes nicely, now I'll never have to clean them again." You have to do it over and over again. And the real art to living is doing it over and over again and not getting bored, seeing that it's never quite exactly the same. If you look at doing dishes as something terrible that you have to do, then it's going to *be* terrible, or you can look at it as cleansing and purification, something in which you can see the results of your action, something completed. There are many times when we don't get the sense of accomplishment that we would like. So why not enjoy the little things when we do get a sense of accomplishment, like doing the dishes? It's our choice to make them dreary tasks or to learn to make them tolerable because there shouldn't be any dead spots in our life. We're not here that long. We don't have any guarantees about how long it's going to be. It behooves us to put as much quality as we can into the time we spend here.

The Tao

I am reluctant to speak about the Tao because it's a paradox to speak about the unspeakable. The Tao is something which can't be explained or written or talked about, but has to be experienced, and so if this section seems confusing, perhaps I'm doing my job right. If it's too clear then I might be too much in my logical, left brain mode to express anything of value. Tao means Way. It means The Way, not a way, but *The* Way, the Way of Harmony. Again, these are words about something wordless. These are labels about experience.

At various times in my private practice I have acquired nicknames from my patients. One of these is "Doctor Analogy" because I spend time telling stories or making analogies to try and convey mind-body principles. I like Zen stories because they are not logical, rational explanations of what's going on but rather point to the nature of reality. One of my favorite Zen stories is of the finger pointing toward the moon. This to me is analogous to books and words and even what I'm saying right now. These words are merely fingers pointing toward the Tao, toward experience. It's easy to get hooked on words. The words are so beautiful or the words are so rational or they fit so well that we become mesmerized by them. It's as if we were standing there staring at someone's finger instead of looking at and appreciating the beauty of the moon. We're mesmerized by the sign or the symbol and we lose sight of what Korzibsky meant by "the word is not the thing." The map is not the territory. The finger is not the moon. The word is not the experience. But I wanted to start this section with a little non-sense about the Tao because that's where everything starts and finishes, and even if these are only narrow or stubby fingers pointing towards experience, experience is still the basis of all that follows.

The Three Levels of Physician in the Orient

In the Oriental concept of the doctor, there are three levels. The first is the person who treats the sick. This is considered the lowest level because it treats people who are already out of touch with the Tao or out of harmony with the cycles of energy in the universe. Treatment on this level includes acupuncture, acupressure, herbs and other similar techniques. These techniques can also be used at a higher level, but the first level is treating sick people.

In the old days in China, a doctor was paid as long as the patient was well. When the patient became ill, the doctor wasn't paid because his job was to maintain the patient's health. If I tried to do that here, I'd go broke because people have many problems which are familially and culturally inculcated from birth.

I believe it's important for the individual to take responsibility for their health rather than depend on someone else. For too long we've looked to health care professionals to take care of us. People have lost their own knowledge and capacity for self-healing. That's what much of holistic health and healing is about, rediscovering ways people can heal themselves and restore their own inner harmony.

The second level of physician in the Orient is the diagnostician. This is the person who does a form of diagnosis in order to tell the patient what potential problems they face and what treatment will help avoid the problem. In Chinese medicine there are four traditional methods of diagnosis. I practice traditional pulse diagnosis, reading the twelve pulses on the radial artery of the wrist. There's also diagnosis by the face, ear, skin, by smell and questioning. There is a sub-system of acupuncture that uses the nose, both for treatment and diagnosis. Diagnosis is considered a higher art because it treats an imbalance before it gets bad. It tunes into a subtle level of the body's functioning. It picks up minor imbalances and slight vibrations, before they can grow into something which causes damage to the organism.

At the third and highest level is the physician who teaches others how to live. This is the person who provides people with the basic principles of health, an understanding of Tai Chi, the Tao, harmony, balance, Yin and Yang, and how to apply them to the body and in one's life. This is also the level of the teacher of Tai Chi Chuan or martial arts who provides people with the techniques they can use themselves. One of the advantages of learning Tai Chi Chuan is that after you take the six months to a year required to learn the form, it's yours. You can continue working on it the rest of your life, and you're not dependent on anyone else. Your teacher is internal, it's your mind-body complex teaching you and taking you to all the succeeding levels possible with the form. Once you learn it, it's yours.

Each of these levels of treatment represents a level of responsibility. The first, where someone else treats you when you are sick, represents the least responsibility. Someone helps do it for you although you must participate. The second level, diagnosis, represents a greater participation because the diagnostician tells you what is *liable* to happen if you do not change your ways to balance with the forces of nature. Then it is your responsibility to *make the changes* that put you in harmony with the Tao, in harmony with the flow of universal energy. In the third method you learn a system from a teacher such as Tai Chi Chuan or Gung Fu. Once you learn the principles from the teacher, it is your responsibility to maintain and apply them, not the teacher's.

Levels of treatment are levels of responsibility, to build up to the point where the person is responsible for their own actions mentally, physically and spiritually. In actual practice, it's necessary to work from all three levels because most people who come to me have been imbued culturally with a system that takes their responsibility for health and gives it away. The needles work directly on the physical body to help the problem, but the dialogue that we have gets the patient to begin taking more responsibility for their physical and emotional body, and their life in general, so they can nurture, balance and work with the energies in their life, and not be dependent on someone to do it for them.

This concept of balancing forces is important, not philo-sophically, but in a real way. There are many things one cannot experience until reaching a basic level of health and self-understanding. Oriental medicine treats the whole person, the whole body; it treats the person's emotions, thoughts, and feel-ings. When the mind and body are balanced, life doesn't just end with individual functioning, but expands to the individual in relation to family, loved ones, friends, co-workers, the world. The concept is not of separation, but of relation; not that we are here and the universe is out there, but that we are part of the universe, and the universe is part of us. Man is the microcosm, the universe is the macrocosm, each reflects the other; they are not separate. Ultimately, they're one. But if we do not recognize harmony in our own selves, how can we recognize or even comprehend harmony external to ourselves?

Meridians

There are fourteen major meridians in classical Chinese medicine. Twelve correspond to the twelve pulses. The other two are special meridians. The Governing Vessel goes along the line of the spine from the base up the back, over the top of the head, and ends at a point in the middle of the roof of the mouth. The other special meridian is the Conception Vessel which starts near the perineum, goes up the middle of the front of the body and ends at the tip of the tongue. This is one reason why Tai Chi Chuan and other meditative forms instruct people to place the tip of the tongue at the roof of the mouth to connect the two major meridians in order to complete what is called the Cosmic Micro-Circuit, so the energy flows in a complete circuit around the front and back midline of the body. Keeping the tongue at the roof of the mouth is important in martial arts also. Anyone who has done sparring or fighting knows it can be painful if the tongue gets caught between the teeth.

The other twelve major meridians correspond to the twelve major pulses: Lung, Large Intestine, Stomach, Spleen, Heart, Small Intestine, Bladder, Kidney, Liver, Gall Bladder, the Pericardium and the Triple Warmer.

The lines that appear on acupuncture charts are the external portions of the meridians. The acupuncture points are the places on the meridian closest to the surface and therefore the easiest way to tap into the energy of that particular meridian. The meridians form a network and the traditional name for this network is Ching-Lo. Ching means the meridians that go up and down; Lo are the ones that go around and connect the other meridians, the points where meridians interesect each other. There are also eight other special meridians in addition to the twelve major ones. But here we'll focus on the twelve major meridians which are energy pathways and that hook into the system we're constantly talking about, Yin and Yang and balance and understanding change in the body. The body is divided into Yin and Yang halves. The upper part is Yang. The lower portion is Yin. The front is Yin. The back is Yang. The meridians are also divided into Yin and Yang. There are three levels of energy in the meridians. There is the lesser Yang, normal Yang, and extreme Yang. There is the lesser Yin, normal Yin, and extreme Yin. The meridians are the pathways that energy travels in the body. There hasn't been any Western scientific verification of this. There once was a man named Bong Han in Korea who did experimentation with injecting a radio-active substance at certain trigger points along the major meridians and then was able to trace and locate deposits of the radio-active material at other traditional acupuncture points. Unfortunately, no one else has been able to replicate his work and he has since disappeared. In a Western scientific sense the results of his study are not considered valid. Nonetheless, for several thousand years, people have been successfully treated for a variety of ailments using this system of balancing energy flows of the body.

There are special points along the meridians known as alarm or source points, where a needle or massage or moxibustion can bring about change in the energy level of that meridian and corresponding organ. A majority of these points are located around the wrist or ankle. The hands and feet are the places where energy changes direction, where energy goes from the inside of the arm through the hand and turns at the fingers and goes up the outside of the arm. The place where energy changes direction is crucial so most of the important source, tonification and sedation points are located around the ankles and feet, wrists and hands. Tonification means adding energy, increasing the flow. Sedation means reducing the flow. The Chinese say that essentially, any health problem is an imbalance in the energy flow of the body. That means too much energy somewhere and not enough somewhere else. Energy is manipulated through the meridians in order to bring about a balance in the state of the person's health.

Moxibustion

Moxibustion is applying heat to acupuncture points or to a needle placed in a particular acupuncture point. Sometimes this is required. Moxa is actually artemisia vulgaris, an herb that is finely shredded and has a certain wooly appearance. It is pressed into little cones and balls which are then either placed on the ends of the needles, or a slice of ginger is placed on the area to be treated, and a cone of moxa is placed on top of the ginger and ignited. It is normally extinguished before it burns entirely and the ginger acts to keep the body from scaring while heat is focused on the particular point. There are also long sticks of compressed moxa which are lit and the glowing end is held a short distance above the skin and the pathway of a meridian is traced to break up an energy blockage. In Auricular Acupuncture, the moxa may be placed on the ends of the needles and ignited, thereby focusing heat through the needle to that point.

It may seem incomprehensible to a Westerner, that if I have a toothache, why stick a needle in my foot? That's because on the foot there may be a point for that particular treatment and half of the meridians travel the entire length of the body. Often the meridian point farthest from the problem is used. For example, the lung meridian emerges on the surface from its connection with the lung, on the chest near the right or left armpit, and travels down the arm to the thumb. Sometimes in treating a lung condition, a point on the thumb will be needled. There is a technique for relieving immediate pain by placing a needle close to the source of the pain. But that is only temporary relief. The most appropriate point farthest from the point of injury or pain is often used.

The main question people ask about acupuncture is, "How does it work?" This reflects our cultural bias in trying to understand everything. The Western perspective is, "What's the theory?" It's necessary to have an intellectual theory or framework in which to place any phenomena, and the phenomena needs to be replicated by other people in accordance with the rules of the theory. The Chinese had their own theories but they were not scientific in the Western sense, so their approach appears as: "Well, it works, let's do it, and think about a theory later." Acupuncture has been in use for (depending on what history you read) anywhere from 3000 to 4500 years, and a substantial amount of empirical evidence has accumulated in that time. However, it doesn't fit with Western perception so it has not been acceptable to the Western mind. It is possible to look at some of the results of acupuncture and understand them in terms of neurological activity. This is a model I primarily use in working with my patients. I explain to them that my theory and way of understanding acupuncture, particular auricular acupuncture, is that the external ear, being a nest of major nerve branches, sends a neurological message to the brain. The brain then interprets this message and acts upon it through the central nervous system. With body acupuncture, many times there are nerves that correspond to the location of acupuncture points and the needle stimulates activity along the pathway of that nerve which will trace back to its source, the brain. The brain then interprets and acts upon that signal and again, through the central nervous system, responds with stimulating the body's repair mechanism. There has recently been scientific verification in a study done with Auricular Acupuncture showing that needles in the ear caused the body to produce enkephalons, powerful pain killers, 200-400 times as powerful as morphine. The body's natural pain killers not only deal with pain, but they allow the body time to repair itself. A study done at the same time with hypnosis did not show the production of enkephalons and this gave the first recent scientific verification that acupuncture actually does something that can be measured. If people continue to probe, I have to tell them I really don't know why, but I know it works. Acupuncture works when applied properly in relation to a person's participation in the process of healing and it is a technique to aid the body in repairing itself. Just as surgery is a technique to correct obvious damage to the body, acupuncture is a technique to correct subtle damage to the body. It works with balancing a person's energy and restoring the natural state of harmony. The participation of the patient is required in order for them to discover for themselves the basic principles of good health and learn methods to balance their own energy and not need the further services of someone else.

Pulses

Essentially all a teacher does is teach you how to learn from yourself. For example, lots of people want to learn about pulse diagnosis because it's fascinating and it's an effective way to tell what's going on in the body. People are always looking for someone to teach them pulse diagnosis, and it's true, you do need to learn certain basics from someone else. But the best thing is to know you can use *your own body* to learn. When I was learning the basics of pulse diagnosis, I woke in the morning and checked my own pulses. There are twelve pulses for the major internal organs, the major energy sub-systems in the body. When you wake up in the morning is a good time to check the pulses because they're fairly calm after sleep. You can check the different pulses and monitor them throughout the day. You can check the kidney pulse before and after a cup of coffee and see the difference. You can check your bladder pulse before and after you go to the bathroom and see the changes. This mind-body system we carry is a great laboratory for experimentation. What a good teacher does is throw you back into your own experience to learn. The best thing anybody can teach you is *how to learn* rather than just teaching you a lot of facts and information.

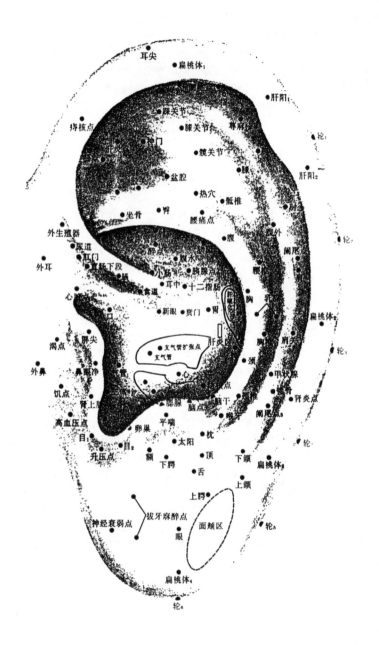

耳尖　　扁桃体₁

肝阳

痔核点　　　膝关节₁　　臀
　　　　　神门　膝关节₂　　　轮
　　　　　　　　髋关节　　　　　肝阳₁₂
　　　　　　盆腔　　膝　　　　　肘
　　　　　　　　热穴　骶椎
　　坐骨　　肾　腰骶点　腹外　　　轮
外生殖器　　　　　腹　　阑尾₃
　尿道　　　　　腹水　腰　　
外耳　肛门　醉点　　胰腺点
　　　直肠下段　　耳中　十二指肠
　　　　食道　　　　　肝炎点　胸　乳
　心　　新眼　贲门　　　胃　　扁桃体₂
　　口　　　　　　肝炎点　　肩关节
涡点　肝尖　　　　　　　　颈　　　轮
外鼻　鼻眼净　支气管扩张点　　甲状腺
饥点　牙上腺　支气管　　　锁骨　肾炎点
高血压点　　　　　腮腺　脑点　脑干　阑尾₂
目₁　　卵巢　平喘　　咽喉　枕
升压点　目₂　太阳　顶　　　轮
　　　额　下腭　舌　下颌　扁桃体₃
　　　　　　　上腭　　上颌
　　　　　　拔牙麻醉点　　　面颊区
神经衰弱点　　　　眼　　　　　轮₈
　　　　　　　　扁桃体₄
　　　　　　　轮₅

36

Auricular Acupuncture

There are over 200 points in the external ear that correspond to every part of the body. I was taught that when the pulses indicate certain things and other methods of diagnosis verify those indications, the needles should be placed in a certain manner to stimulate the body to repair itself. Other than my own tentative explanation that there's a neurological connection from the ear to the brain and the brain processes information and passes it on through the central nervous system, there is no "official" explanation of how Auricular Acupuncture works.

Auricular Acupuncture has been developed in the last forty years in China, and then, more recently, in France by Dr. Norgier. It is fast, safe, and effective. In Auricular Acupuncture, the needles only need to be left in for approximately 20 or 30 minutes. The needles need only go in a short distance because of the tremendous number of major nerve branches located in the ear. To measure the effect of acupuncture on the body, pulse diagnosis is used.

The needles go in and send a nerve impulse directly to the brain. The brain interprets and acts on that impulse and affects the appropriate part of the body through the central nervous system. The change in the pulse can be detected in a matter of moments. If there is not a sufficient change, another point should be used or perhaps a re-evaluation should occur as to what points are to be used in that particular situation.

Martial Arts-Healing Arts

Martial Arts/Healing Arts

Introduction

This chapter will be a brief overview of the relationship between the Martial Arts and the Healing Arts. In the process of writing this book it became evident that to do full justice to the interrelations of meditation, healing, philosophy and the practice of the Martial Arts would require a book in itself. This will be accomplished with the publication of *Martial Arts/Healing Arts* (Auricle Press) , in the near future. In the meantime, I want to provide some general information on the subject.

The martial arts, the meditative arts, and the healing arts all go together. When you combine a martial art that develops the body-mind coordination and you have a meditational art which develops the mind and the spirit in coordination, these together *are* a healing art. They develop body, mind and spirit in coordination, and what form of healing does not have these elements? To me, that's what healing is: getting coordination, communication, energy flow, identity and understanding within the body, mind and spirit.

Background and History

The path of the Martial Arts/Healing Arts parallels that of Buddhism from its beginnings in India, on to Tibet, China, Japan and throughout all of Asia. Tracing this path is to observe the process of change at work in the blending of philosophy and practice within each culture along the way.

When Buddhism went from India to Tibet, it also went from India to China. When Buddhism reached China, it came in contact with Taoism, the natural, philosophical system of China, dealing with an understanding of the Tao, Yin-Yang, and the nature of change. Out of the two (Buddhism and Taoism) came Chan teachings. Chan is the Chinese word for Dhyana, which is the Sanskrit word for meditation.

Chan teachings went from China to Japan and came in contact with Shintoism, a Japanese natural religion, similar to Taoism, and what developed in Japan was Zen Buddhism. Zen is the Japanese translation of Chan, which is the Chinese translation of the Indian word Dhyana, all of which relate to the state of meditation. The person who carried Buddhism to China was Bodhidharma, and the legend says that when he came to China, he taught that meditation should be done facing a wall as it is done in Chan or Zen practice. He sat facing the wall for nine years before he reached Enlightenment. He found the monks couldn't sit for long. They fell asleep because their bodies were not in good shape, so he taught them exercises. Presumably these were exercises he had learned in India and used himself, and this is purportedly the origin of the 18 forms of Lohan, or 18 movements which were taught to the monks to help keep them in physical shape since they didn't do physical labor. Already we can see the relationship between mind and body in this. You can't just sit and develop your mind. You can't just work and exercise your body. You have to do both. So the monks would train in the martial arts and then they would sit and train in the art of meditation.

The 18 movements, then, became the basis of the system known as Shaolin, the hard style, the external style, perhaps to balance the internal-ness of meditation. This was one of the early forms of what is called "Gung-Fu" (Cantonese) or "Kung-Fu" (the Mandarin pronounciation). Gung-Fu means "work well done" or "doing well."

In Japan, the martial arts were known by many names. Japan had its own warrior class, the Samurai. Their hand fighting systems later became popularly known as Karate. Just as there was an exchange of information between the scholars of Tibet and India, knowledge and techniques also travelled back and forth between Japan and China. There have been periods of animosity between the two countries, but there were also periods of cultural exchange.

As you can see, there's a history of the martial arts flowing through the East — from India to China, from China to Japan, permeating Asia. This is true for the meditational arts as well.

Each of the indigenous religious, philosophical systems, like Hinduism, Taoism, Shintoism and Bon (in Tibet), had their own methodology of healing which was complementary to and expanded by the contact with the new meditational arts and philosophical practices of Buddhism.

In my practice, the prime focus is on the Chinese concepts and practices of the martial arts and the healing arts, but having also studied Indian philosophy and Japanese arts, I am aware of how they overlap and inter-relate.

Tai Chi Chuan – Introduction

Are any of you familiar with Tai Chi Chuan? It's a Chinese form of exercise and meditation, it's movement done very slowly and gracefully. It takes about 1/2 hour to go through the whole form which has 108 movements. It has many different levels, which I'll talk about a little because I have both studied martial arts and taught martial arts for many years. Tai Chi Chuan is a way to exercise the entire physical body, all the joints and all the ligaments. It's excellent for the cardio-vascular system, and it's a gentle exercise which is also calming to the mind. When people are doing martial arts exercises, they're supposed to be mentally present as well as physically doing the exercises. Often I have patients come into my clinic who have been doing physical exercise and have hurt themselves because they were thinking about shopping or last night's dinner, and their mind was somewhere else and they weren't paying attention to what they were doing with their body. In Eastern methods the concept is that we operate more effectively and more efficiently if we have our mind *and* body in the same place at the same time. Much of Oriental health care is really training people to take better care of themselves. It's to avoid being dependent on somebody or something out there to take care of your health, and taking more responsibility for yourself. That's why people learn Tai Chi Chuan. It takes six months to a year to learn the form, and then it's yours. You can practice it every day and doing it once or twice a day will keep your physical body in good health. It will also help your mental health by providing a time when you don't have to think about anything. Much of Oriental medicine is predicated on the mind and body working together. Modern brain research has created a tremendous amount of interest and information about the two hemispheres of the brain. We have one side that's logical, rational and does the linear thinking and the language part; and the other side that's holistic, intuitive, musical and artistic. What's needed to be a whole person is both sides functioning properly and the corpus collosum that connects them acting as a channelling device to enable us to use whatever mode of expression is appropriate rather than always being logical and rational or always being emotional, when neither is totally appropriate for all situations.

Have any of you ever watched Star Trek or have children who watch Star Trek on television? Well, the analogy with that is that we couldn't all be just like Mr. Spock ("But Captain, it's not logical"). On the other hand, we can't always be Dr. McCoy ("But for God's sake Jim, there are people on that planet"). We have to balance the two, and that's part of Oriental medicine and part of Oriental art.

Tai Chi Chuan – Self Defense

If we have to think about something, we're slow. The martial arts are a great way of discovering this. The first time I sparred with my current Tai Chi Chuan teacher, I didn't really want to fight. But I saw that in order to learn from him it was necessary for me to do that, and so one day I sparred. I sparred with one of the students who was a machinist and very strong, and a good fighter. He had some knowledge of boxing as well. While we were sparring, he hit me in the face and my eyes started watering and my nose ran, and it hurt; it was very painful. The pain of it stopped me. It shocked me. I thought, "Wow, that really hurts."

In the time it took me to stop and think about it, he hit me four more times right in the face. After that I didn't make the mistake any more of stopping to think. The mind is too slow; the body is much faster. When we're really conscious, we can react with the intelligence of our body and bypass the thinking mind.

When you're sparring is not the time to stop and think, "Am I holding my elbow right?" It's the time to find out whether you're holding your elbow right by whether you block the punch or whether you get hit. You don't have time to think about it.

When I read Gurdjieff's work years ago, I thought, "Gee, thinking is really fast. Why, we can think real quick. How can he say that the instinctive center, the moving center, is faster than the thinking center?" But when I got into sparring, I recognized the truth of what he had said. I experienced it. I intellectually read the words earlier, but until I had the physiological experience it didn't really become my knowledge. I didn't own it. I think what's really essential in the martial and healing arts is knowing, not just intellectually, but owning. Then nobody can take it away from you because it's yours. It's something you possess. In fact, it's not just something you possess, it's yours, it's you.

We can read all the books we want about something, but reading books doesn't make knowledge ours. It's how we practice it; it's incorporating it into our lives. Martial arts is a good example. If you ever need to defend yourself, it doesn't matter how good your teacher is, the point is how much have you absorbed of your teacher's training and converted into your own skill? When push comes to shove, it's what you can do; it's how well you think; it's how well you feel; it's how accurately you move; it's how you use the things you have practiced. You can't say, "Hey, look buddy, my teacher is really great." You'd get punched in the nose. You have to be able to respond appropriately and properly to the situations that are presented to you in reality, not just in your imagination.

In Tai Chi Chuan the saying is, "Where the mind goes, the body follows." It's a way to try to get people to understand that we need to use the imagination to help train the body, but the body has to follow; we have to do it with our bodies. We have to use the things that we load our heads with, and most people are so top-heavy it's ridiculous. Most people are totally out of touch with their actual center of gravity, both mentally and physically. The physical center of gravity is about two inches below the navel, not up in our heads. Yet, we think so much and we're such a verbal, visual, auditory society that we

46

think our heads are all there is to us. It's not. The head is a small part of the body. Sure, it houses the brain, but you can't separate the brain from the body and the body from the brain. We make a whole person and all our parts have to function well together. If we move our center too high, we throw ourselves off balance, and we lose our ability to function as balanced, harmonious, creative, intelligent human beings.

Other Approaches to Healing

Other Approaches to Healing

Group Dynamics

Auricular Acupuncture can be done in a group and this gives treatment a dynamic aspect. I think this is what I like best about it. Furthermore, there is a practical, financial consideration. Group treatments keep costs down and in a day of rising prices, it's important to keep health care as reasonable as possible. With body treatments, you can only treat one person at a time because of the necessity of disrobing and because people have to lie down and this takes up more space. You need a padded table or comfortable surface for the patient to lie on. By having people sit around a table, in groups of up to six people, the cost is kept down. It doesn't mean treatments need be done like an assembly line. I can spend time with people and if it's necessary to work individually with someone, it can still be done. But in most cases it's best as soon as possible to get a person into a group session to re-integrate them socially from the isolated conditions of their illness.

People who have had pain or physical problems for a long time tend to become more and more restricted in their contacts with others. They get involved in a negative feedback system. Once again, it's Yin and Yang. Illness can make you too Yin, too inward, focusing mainly on pain, discomfort or whatever the particular imbalance is. During treatment, a person initially will feel better because the treatment will help the body rebalance itself. But since they've been dealing with pain for so long, patients might not trust feeling better even though they are recovering. They might not believe or accept it. But in a group treatment, sitting around the table with other people, someone may say, "Hey, you're looking better. Your color is different. Your face looks different. What have you done?" When there's external verification of what someone feels internally, they begin to think, "Well, I was *feeling* better and then he said that I *looked* better, maybe I *am* getting better." Then their energy starts to work in a more creative way as they become open to the possibility of getting well. Whenever a condition actually begins to improve, we are once again aware of the major premise of Oriental medicine, that our natural state is health, and the physician's job is to help remove the blocks to that natural condition so energy can flow properly and we can get back on the road again, taking responsibility for our own lives and health.

It's not as simple as putting six people in a room and sticking needles in them because there's a dynamic interplay in the group dialogue. In one-to-one therapy, one of the disadvantages is transference, when the patient becomes too attached to the therapist. Group treatment avoids this because everyone participates, everyone is involved. It's not just the therapist who is all-wise and all-knowing. It is everyone getting in touch with their own knowledge, with their own wisdom.

With a group, there's an ebb and flow, a give and take. I don't know everything. I learn from my patients, they learn from me; they learn from the other patients, we teach each other. The value of the individual's treatment is magnified by the interplay of energy between the participants in a group. Also, when working on a one-to-one basis, there tends to be a phenomenon I call tracking. If I have a series of sessions with Patient A and a series of sessions with Patient B, Patient A and I will have a particular track. Perhaps Patient A is a writer, so we will talk about books, authors, publishing and things that we have in common and relate them to the healing process. But with Patient B who is, let's say, a mother with a small child, I might talk about the basic principles of health, in relation to children, nutrition and family relationships. So there is a different track for Patient B.

When we have a group in which both Patient A and Patient B are participating, something special happens. In talking to Patient B about raising children and nutrition, something valuable to Patient A may come up which could never have been shared in an individual session because of the tracking phenomena. I'm not smart enough to know what is going to be most valuable to every patient every time. The group allows for a spontaneous procedure so that in talking with Patient A about publishing, an insight or analogy or parallel may be provided to Patient B that will trigger growth and development.

I have seen wonderful changes occur in the treatment room when people get together and relax. In Chinese, the word for relaxation is "sung." The Chinese say real relaxation is like a cat patiently waiting for a mouse. If the cat falls asleep, it misses the mouse. The cat is also not on the edge of its chair waiting for the mouse, because then it would get exhausted and wouldn't be able to react fast enough when the mouse appears. The cat is *relaxed*. It's not using any unnecessary tension, but it is aware, it is conscious of the changes in the situation so that it can, in a mirror-like fashion, respond and react appropriately to what happens without necessarily having to think about it.

Theory of Relationships

I love stories and drawings and diagrams because they're often ways to trick ourselves into acknowledging things we might not have seen before. It's like a joke that makes you laugh at something, and then you realize that you do the same thing. But we laugh at it first because it's out there, outside of us. This is the Tai Chi diagram:

Tai Chi means Supreme Ultimate. As a martial art, it's called Tai Chi Chuan because Chuan means fist. What this diagram represents is a way of perceiving reality as two forces which balance and complement each other. It shows the mutual inter-penetration of energies. The Chinese perspective is that, yes, there are two forces like day and night, hot and cold, hard and soft, male and female, but they don't conflict. There isn't a hard, straight line between the two. They're opposite, but they're shaped the same. They're opposite but not opposed. Each one contains at its very core the seed of the other to show the relationship between the two. They are connected rather than two parts that just happen to be next to each other. This is a great model for anything. If you want to look at a process to find whether there's harmony in it, use this model. See if there's a balance of forces, a balance of energy.

Here's an example from the martial arts: In doing any kind of movement, you always want to work from your center and when you're putting energy out in the martial sense, you want to not over-extend yourself. If you over-extend yourself, you'll lose your own sense of balance, you'll uproot yourself, not the other person. Your opponent won't have to do anything if you extend beyond your center of gravity. On the other hand, if you yield too far, you can uproot yourself as well. You want to find a way to move back and forth without uprooting yourself by being too aggressive, and without destroying your own integrity by being too yielding. If you meet force with force, it's going to be which force has more mass behind it, which one is faster, which one has more energy. But if you work with a circle you can take any negative energy that's directed towards you and re-direct it — you don't have to meet it head on. You can take control of that energy and send it back. You can also apply this to relationships. A real relationship has a balance to it, and if you find that there's something wrong in a relationship, then see if you're not putting enough energy into it, or if you're putting in too much energy. Either you're being too aggressive or too passive.

I have what I call the Howland Theory of Relationships and it will be demonstrated by these little stick figures:

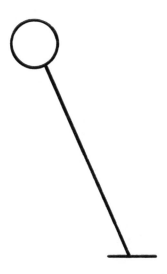

This is an example of what makes a poor relationship, that is, when you're not very much in touch with your center and you're looking for something out there. This is where the mind gets too far ahead of the body. A Tai Chi Chuan saying is, "where the mind goes the body follows." Well, *if* the body follows, that's OK because then the mind and the body meet in a sort of harmony that will make it possible for them to help each other. But if the mind gets too far ahead of the body, the body says, "What about me?" And the body is left behind. That's what happens sometimes, the mind gets out there ahead of the body and so the person is teetering and about to fall over. They're unbalanced. They're always looking for something. You know this kind of person. You see them every day. And people like this are attracted to anyone who has any sort of center or grounding and looks like this:

What happens is the person who's looking outside themself wants to get together with one of these, so this is what the relationship looks like:

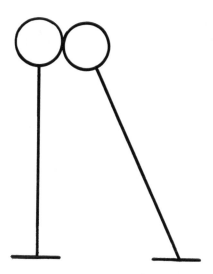

Well, it's doomed. It's not going to last because this creates too much pressure at the top and this person will finally say, "Hey, I'm being knocked off center by this constant pressure." Also, there's not a great deal of contact because there's communication on one level and their real bases are in different places.

Then the other alternative is if two of these people get together, and that looks like this:

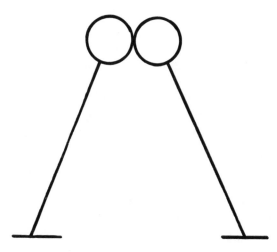

Then again there's only contact at the top and these two people find that they're even farther apart. What really makes for a good relationship is this:

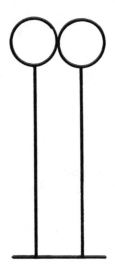

because there's more contact, more communication. It's not dependency, not needing something from the other that you can provide yourself. That is, being grounded, self-assured and balanced. A psychologist friend of mine once did a survey of couples in relationships and asked, "Which are you more afraid of, entrapment or rejection?" And in each case, one person said entrapment and the other said rejection. The people who were afraid of entrapment were being cool; they wanted to keep their distance. Well, two people who are being like that are so cool they won't get anywhere near each other, right? They never really make contact:

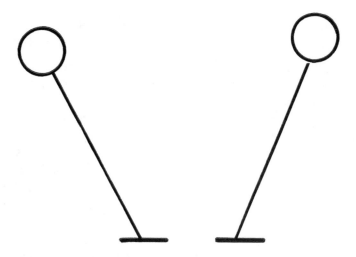

And two people who are afraid of rejection, cling, and they cling to each other so much they smother each other in the relationship. There's a certain kind of bizarre balance that goes on, in terms of her study. Take the principles of Yin and Yang and apply them to these situations. If it's a good principle it will work on different levels.

Maps – Other Ways

I'd like to talk a little about maps of the body which show inter-relationships. One of the reasons Auricular Acupuncture is so effective is that the ear is a map of the body's energy. We use over 200 points on the external ear, front and back, 200 points which relate to every part of the body. The ear is a homunculae; it's like a fetus upside down, so the relationship of the points are similar to the relationships in the body. For example, the points for the trachea are near the points for the top of the lung and the points for the esophagus are near the points for the upper part of the stomach.

It's similar to the way the organs are positioned in the body. The ear is a powerful map of the body, but there are many maps and that's what's interesting about diagnostic techniques. Many cultures use different methods that provide the same basic information. Our human mind-body system is remarkable. It tells us in hundreds of ways what is going on at any particular moment *if* we are willing to spend the time learning how to read the maps.

Reflexology works with feet and hands and can, to a certain extent, be used to discover and alleviate imbalances throughout the body. Iridology is a diagnostic system observing the iris of the eye and the changes in that special form of tissue. Those changes reflect changes in the internal conditions of various parts of the body.

In acupuncture there is a sub-system for the hand that can be used to treat most of the body. There's also a sub-system for the nose. These maps help the diagnostician discover where the imbalance is. If you use more than one map, you can check out one system, find out what the problem is according to that and then check another system to confirm and refine the diagnosis. There are four traditional methods of diagnosis in Chinese medicine. Pulse diagnosis is the best known and most widely practiced. There is also diagnosis by the ear which is a very effective way to determine what's going on in the body. You can diagnose by appearance, by the color of the face and hands, the tone of voice and movement of the body. You can diagnose by asking questions to determine life patterns and also by examination of urine and feces to determine the balance or imbalance in the patient's system. The reason for all these techniques is simple: the more accurate the diagnosis, the more successfully the dysfunction can be treated and the person can return to a normal state of health.

The more accurate the diagnosis, the simpler the treatment. Simplicity of treatment also means using the least amount of intervention that does the job. For example, I use three levels of stimulation. One is placing the needle in the ear, two is stimulating the needle by twirling it in a clockwise or counter-clockwise direction manually, and three is hooking the needles to an electrical stimulator from China, and having the person gradually adjust the amount of stimulation. The electrical stimulator provides a vibrating or tingling sensation and has an effect similar to that of me continuously twirling the needles.

I use the least amount of energy to do the job. If manually stimulating the needles will do it, then there's no need for the machine. If just the needles being placed in position stimulates the body to say, "Oh yeah, I can do that," then there's no need for over-stimulation. There are also times when needles are not appropriate. Usually, children should not need to be needled. Their problems can generally be treated by first massaging the ears, second, massaging the feet, and finally, massaging along the spine. This will usually stimulate the body to repair itself. Children don't need the strong stimulation of needles because their bodies haven't learned as many bad habits as adults' bodies. They're closer to their natural state and can bounce back faster when impaired.

When a woman is pregnant, one has to be very cautious with acupuncture because it is quite effective for delivery. Certain points can't be needled during pregnancy. When a person is at an advanced age the needles sometimes are not necessary or may be too strong, depending on the individual's health habits during their lifetime.

Mind-Body Relationships

I haven't found anything that is totally a mind problem or totally a body problem. So far everyone who's come to my office has brought both mind and body with them. In many physiological problems, there is a psychological antecedent. For example, ulcers. Nobody's born with ulcers. You're not just walking down the road and suddenly lightening strikes and you have ulcers. Ulcers are created as a result of what we eat, how we eat, and how we deal with tension and stress. They're created from habit patterns so the needles can stimulate the body to repair itself but if we don't do something about the mental end of it, the habitual end of it, we will re-create the problem again.

The mind can exert a great deal of control *over* the body, however, it's more important to find ways to get the mind and body working *together*. Our culture tends to be too mind oriented. That's another reason why people breathe in the upper chest. We act as if our heads were the most important part of our body. We tend to think it's the center of our being. It's not. Our physiological center is just below the navel. The head is just *part* of what we are. Many of the problems in Western culture can be viewed from the perspective of mind interpreting the body's experience. The mind should do its job and the body should do its job. Many times people try to use their minds to run the body and over-control their bodies. We get lots of strokes for mind stuff in our culture and so more of us tend to have our energy there. For example, I have a delightful friend who has a problem with compulsive eating. He eats to feed his head, not his body. Food is for the body, not just the head. But what my friend does is say, "God, that looks great. That smells great. Umm. That tastes good." And his head is saying, "More, more." And his body is saying, "No! No!" But he's not listening to the body. He's letting the head tell the rest of his body what's going to happen. There needs to be a balance between the mind and the body. We're upside down in a way, if we live only in our heads.

Psychology of the Body

A lot of people don't understand how intelligent the body is. It's the mind that does the talking so we tend to place value on that level of communication. The body is really smart but just because it can't tell us things with words we tend not to validate its information. But its information is just as worthwhile and often more appropriate than what comes through our head. In Western culture, most people filter their body experiences through their heads so a lot of their information about their body is channelled through the intellect and it's not necessarily as valid or as good as direct information. The body stores things. Many times something happens that we can't handle intellectually, and since we don't process it, we store it. In techniques like Rolfing, people can suddenly have a flashback to something that happened to them at an earlier time in their life. The body remembers experiences and feelings. A big part of any health practice is understanding it's important for the body to do the body's job and the mind to do the mind's job and for the two of them to cooperate.

Male-Female Energy

I'd say 80% of my patients are women and there are many reasons for this. One is that women are more open about their problems, and another is that women are more in touch with their feelings, more aware of their bodies. Another factor is that we live in a male dominated culture which tends to cause a lot more problems for women. But it's not a question of male or female dominance. The best analogy I can think of is, it doesn't matter if you nail your right foot to the floor and run around in a circle or you nail your left foot to the floor and run around in a circle counter-clockwise. Either way won't get you anywhere. There's a balancing that needs to go on between maleness and femaleness in each and every one of us and not just in the culture. The culture, in many ways, reflects a distorted functioning of the hemispheres of the brain, a distorted understanding of what a human being is. I just happen to be male on the outside, but I'm a human being, and I can be sensitive and nurturing and like poetry and flowers and cooking as well as martial arts and classic cars. You've got to be a whole person and that's what this book refers you to — wholeness, balancing maleness and femaleness. In the United States men die much younger than women because of abnormal work pressures, poor diet and poor exercise. That leaves many women who have been married a number of times or who have lost several husbands and who have to take care of children and support themselves. Then they have to learn how to get in touch with their left hemisphere, their male side, their ability to think logically and rationally and take care of business and fulfill all their responsibilities. To be a whole human being means balancing those two sides, getting them to work together.

William Blake wrote a book called, "The Marriage of Heaven and Hell," and it's basically about alchemy or the internal marriage, learning to balance the two hemispheres, the two sides. Instead of labelling these forces good and evil ("I'm good and I have to wipe out evil." "I'm evil and I have to wipe out good."), we can recognize that they each have a common source and that in a way they create each other. It's not necessary to struggle because there is a common source of energy, and we can get in touch with that common source. Which brings me to this drawing:

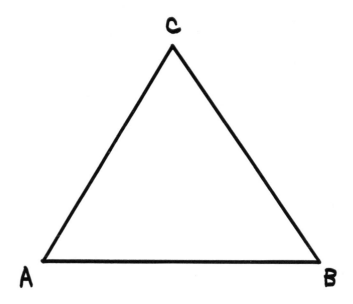

another model for being-in-the-world, and you could call Angle A the mind and Angle B the body, and Angle C the spirit of the common source or body energy.

The Five Elements of Vitality

The Five Elements of Vitality

Introduction

The Chinese look at energy as having five elements which go together to create the quality of our Chi or energy or vital force. I'll just briefly mention them, but they're all worth learning about. One of these we don't have any control over, and four of them we can control. The one we can't control is ancestral karma, and that relates to DNA and RNA, the genetic aspect of our being. The first element we can control is food: what we eat, when we eat, how we eat. The next element is breath. Just as a car has to have the proper air-fuel mixture, we need to breathe to balance and metabolize our food intake. Our breath has a lot to do with the quality of our life experience. Once you build a body with food and breath, the next element is physical exercise, how you move through space and time, how you use your body. Most people either don't get enough exercise or over-do it. And the last of the five elements is mental exercise. If we only use our body in certain limited ways we develop fixed patterns of physcial behavior. Since the body and mind reflect each other, we can simultaneously develop rigid patterns of mental behavior. We need to exercise our minds as well as our bodies. Whenever there's a problem with your overall energy, you should examine these five elements: food, breath, physical exercise, mental exercise, and ancestral karma, or heredity.

Look at what you eat and when you eat and how you eat, and look at it in terms of this: Is there something you're eating too much of? Is there something you're not eating? Look at all the little balances within each element and then look at your breathing. People breathe too much in the upper chest and not enough in the lower abdomen. The lower abdomen is meant to be flexible; the upper chest is not meant to be as flexible. If you're breathing in the upper chest, you're only using about 75% of your lung capacity, which means you're not getting enough oxygen in your system and not only is your circulation poor, but your brain doesn't work as well. You're not taking very good care of your body if your brain isn't working properly. The brain works better if it gets more oxygen, so examine your breathing and then look at your physical exercise. Once you've got a body, what do you do with it? Do you sit all day? What forms of exercise do you do in order to circulate your energy? And then how do you circulate your mental energy? If you think in the same patterns all the time, maybe take a break and look at your life with a different perspective. Look at your relationships from the other person's perspective; try and see it from the other side as an exercise in flexibility. The mind, the thinking part, is an incredible piece of equipment. Mentally you can create anything you want. It's like a blackboard. You can create something in your head or you can wipe it out if you don't like it. But the things we think about are the things we often do, so it benefits us to exercise more control over our thoughts. Ancestral karma, food, breath, physical exercise and mental exercise combine to determine the quality of our Chi or energy.

Ancestral Karma

One of the five elements the Chinese believed we didn't have much control over is called ancestral karma or ancestral Chi. What it means is heredity, DNA and RNA. It means the characteristics we've inherited, like the color of our hair, the color of our eyes, the aspects we don't control, although it's interesting to note that in medicine in the last ten to fifteen years many things that were considered hereditary have been discovered to be culturally or familially inculcated. Allergies and asthma can be more psychological than physiological in that our bodies can learn them from the people we're around.

I've had a number of patients with allergies and asthma who came to me because nothing had ever helped them. In the process of treatment they would casually reminisce and talk about their families and they often would hit upon one relative, a grandmother or grandfather or an aunt or uncle who they'd been attached to and I could see that when they talked about that person, they changed. I had a number of patients who experienced "miraculous" cures because they realized some of their attachments from childhood were more than just being fond of someone. Their bodies had actually learned an illness or mimicked the pattern of someone else.

That's one reason why cancer and heart disease and obesity tend to go in families, not just because of the genes, or DNA and RNA, but because your body absorbs patterns from the people you're around. For example, if you repeatedly tell a child they're stupid, no matter how smart they are, the child, in most cases, is going to act as if they were stupid. Children respond to the authority figures in their lives. I had a friend who was a very sensitive and talented artist but never trusted her ability because her parents always told her she was no good at art. There was a conflict between her urge to be an artist and what she had been brought up to believe. Many conditions that used to fall into the ancestral karma category are now falling out of it into areas where people have to take responsibility.

There's a book called *Scripts People Live By,* by Claude Steiner (Phantom Books), which says that children at a young age find how they're supposed to live and die. If somebody meaningful to them had cancer and died, then they frequently chose that as a way to die. Those scripts can be unlearned once you figure out where you got your script. You can spend the rest of your life living that script or you can write your own.

The genetic element was said by the Chinese to be one over which we had little or no control. Concerning the other four, we have two choices: We can either be actively involved in keeping the elements in balance, or we can give up conscious control and our ability to choose.

Food

The first element we can control is food. This has to do with what we eat, when we eat and how much we eat. It has to do with the basic building blocks of our body. The human mind-body complex is an amazing piece of equipment capable of synthesizing almost anything it needs out of basic raw materials, the building blocks of nutrition. However if we don't provide it with those basic elements, it has to run on reserves stored up from the past. When it exhausts those, and we don't replenish the stocks, then we run into a problem. We need a balance in our food intake. In relation to food, again, look at it from the perspective of Yin and Yang.

Too much food relative to exercise and we gain unnecessary weight. Statistically, there are over 40 million people in this country who are from ten to twenty pounds overweight. We eat as if we were living more actively than we are. The formula is simple. If we eat too much, we need to exercise more. If we don't exercise much, we should cut down on our eating. It's a Yin-Yang balance. We don't operate from a perspective of our whole body. We operate from a perspective of tastes, olfactory pleasure, and enjoyment. We eat to feed our heads, not our bodies. We don't eat as whole people. We eat to satisfy the parts. And so, in food, a balance is required.

We also have to look at what we eat, to see that there's a balance, that we get green and yellow vegetables, fruits, and the right amount of protein. Again, not too much, not too little.

When I work with people, I have them write down everything they eat for three days. I tell them not to think of it in terms of being graded, but just to be honest. You have to be honest with yourself and honest with someone who's trying to assist you at a particular point in your development. After they write down for three days what they eat, I take a look at it. Generally, I notice two things: Once again, Yin and Yang. The yin part is a lack of something. Usually it's either a lack of vegetables or a lack of fresh fruit. Secondly, there's usually a Yang condition from too much of something. The too muches are usually either too much in the way of sweets (sugars, candies, chocolates) or too much in the way of starches (breads, pastas, bulks), or also, too much in the way of salt. The body needs very little salt. Yet our taste has been conditioned to want greater amounts of salt than the body can process. This, along with other things, contributes to hardening of the arteries and other circulatory and internal problems.

Food needs to be balanced in relation to how we burn it up, what we take in, and when we eat it. The body does internal repair work at night. If we take in food just before we go to bed, the crew inside the body says, "Hey, we were just about to knock off and punch out, and here comes all this food to be processed. We're gonna have to do something with this. What's going on here?" The crew has to stay awake. They grumble, they complain; they can't do their regular jobs because there's all this food to be processed and some of them have already gone home. So they say, "Okay, there's nothing much we can do. We gotta put it in storage." Guess where storage is? Storage is around the middle, and then that has to wait for a time when you exercise enough to justify breaking into those storage rooms. Who knows when that will be? Also, if you eat a lot, that night crew gets a little disgruntled because they have

73

to work overtime and not necessarily get paid that much in terms of good health and good circulation. They send a runner up to the brain and say, "Hey, give this turkey a bad dream, something to let him know this isn't a good idea." Dreams often give us an indication of what is going on in the body. Dreams give us a different perspective, a different view saying what we need and what we're doing. But many times we don't remember them or don't think they're important or don't pay attention to them.

Understanding requires effort but it's well worth it in terms of self-knowledge and self-awareness.

Breath

The second controllable element of Chi is breath. The Chinese say, look at how a baby breathes. A baby breathes entirely into the lower abdomen. If you watch them their whole abdomen swells up and you can actually feel their breathing along their back. There's a saying that a baby breathes from their belly, in middle age a person breathes from their chest, in old age a person breathes from their throat, and a dying man's last breath is from his lips. We tend to let our breath go up, and if you keep it down, if you keep breathing into the lower abdomen, you'll live longer and you'11 live a lot healthier.

Every philosophical system that I have studied focuses on breath and its importance. There's a dynamic interplay between inhaling and exhaling, but it's not only that, it's the quality. It's how effectively we breathe. Our lungs have a particular capacity, and most of us use perhaps 70% of it. We tend to stick the chest out and hold the tummy in, which is just the opposite of the way our body is constructed. The rib cage is semi-moveable; it's not designed to be totally flexible. We put abnormal pressure and strain on the upper portion of the body by breathing up into the chest too much. The lower abdomen, the solar plexus area, is designed to be flexible. Not only does it expand when we inhale but it also must contract when we exhale to fully evacuate the lungs. Most of us breathe backwards. If we only breathe in the chest we create a Yang condition, too much energy in the upper portion of the body. That contributes to neck and shoulder tension, headaches, shortness of breath, and a tendency to get over-emotional because of a lack of oxygen in the system.

On the other hand, if we don't move our lower abdomen, our internal organs, our viscera, don't get the proper exercise they need. Also, chest breathers tend to have rigid diaphragms, which is not healthy. The body needs to be elastic and flexible. That's what makes things work properly. Inhaling, exhaling, flexing, extending. It's movement; it's dynamic. If we don't breathe into the lower abdomen, the diaphragm tends to get rigid and that causes many internal problems. If we do breathe into tho lower abdomen, we use more of our lung capacity and provide more oxygen. We then circulate more oxygen throughout the system, which means our brain works better, our cells get replaced faster, our body works more efficiently. Food provides the building blocks, the repairing and regenerative materials for the body. Breathing circulates it, moves it around. If we breathe poorly and inefficiently, the supply lines slow down and necessary repairs are not made. That means illness is created, we become weaker and the lines of communication are down in the body. Breathing helps us circulate our energy and get oxygen where it needs to go, it helps filter blood and remove toxins and waste materials from our body so that we're constantly rebuilding and repairing and keeping the body dynamic.

When the viscera are not exercised it means that waste materials can coat the wall of the intestines. Deposits build up until there are problems with evacuation of waste materials. Toxins and harmful substances can then accumulate in the body and stay in the system too long, and you can actually poison yourself. An enema forcibly cleans the intestines. But breathing into the lower abdomen massages and moves around the intestines so that they're *naturally* active. When accumulated deposits are removed from the intestinal walls, the intestines can function in a normal and healthy way. Many problems can be avoided by proper exercise and breathing. Breathing is an energizing exercise when done relaxed and deep into the lower abdomen, not overstressing the chest, but filling the lungs from the bottom up. If we start at the top, we never fill the bottom, so we have to start filling the lungs from the bottom up.

The breath is an important way to extend and augment the value of the energy provided by proper food intake.

Physical Exercise

The third area is physical exercise. Once we have built the body out of food and circulated energy from that food through our breath, we come to physical exercise, which is moving the physical body through time and space. It's extremely important how we use the body once we have built it, once it has been constructed. Unfortunately, our culture is such that people breathe poorly, breathe too little, eat too much, and then don't exercise. When people worked on the land or did physical exercise their food got burnt up and used more effectively. They had to breathe harder, so it meant they used their lungs more fully in order to get their work done. More oxygen was provided for the efficient combustion of food and distribution of food elements. Physical exercise contributed to good sleep, good appetite, and good health. But now, how much exercise do people get? Look at all the people jogging and running and playing racquet ball and tennis and various other exercises to try to compensate for this.

The average person gets up in the morning, sits at a table and eats breakfast. Then they sit in a car or bus or subway to go to work. They sit in an office and do their work. Then they go to lunch. They sit down and eat their food. They go back and sit in the office. They get tired in the afternoon because they've eaten more food than they have burnt off, and then after they finish work they sit in their car or the bus or the subway and go home, and sit down and read their paper and sit at the table and eat their dinner, and sit in front of the TV and then go to bed.

There are many muscles and ligaments and tendons in the body which never get exercise. We have to keep coming back to an understanding of the body as a unit; it is all connected. If we don't exercise parts of it, it has an effect on the whole; an effect on the total organism. Many of the exercises which people do exercise only *parts* of the body. It's important to try and exercise *all* of the body.

When people worked in the fields and did manual labor, they learned to use their back, not just their legs. People have gotten away from that. Jobs do not require physical exercise anymore, so they've forgotten what it's like. They have also lost touch with the good feeling of having their body work as a unit. This is where the martial arts have a distinct advantage in that effective systems of martial arts, like Tai Chi Chuan, were designed to use the whole body. Scholars, who sat around reading and studying, could do something that would exercise all the muscles, bones, ligaments, and tendons in order to keep their physical body as healthy as possible, considering their lifestyle. How we move our body through space and time and the quality of our exercise should be looked at from the perspective of Yin and Yang.

People who start exercise programs tend to do way too much at first, and then nothing at all. What really works and lasts is a balance. Doing a certain amount of exercise every day, and working on it, gradually building up what you can do. Also, a balanced *amount* of exercise, not doing too much one time and not enough the next, but balancing it. It's much better to do five minutes every day for a month. You'll get more out of doing that than half an hour one day, fifteen minutes the next, nothing for three days, and then forty minutes, and then nothing for a week. Consistency. It's like breathing. We can't say, "I'm going to do all my breathing for the next three days today so I won't need to breathe for two days." It doesn't work that way. We have to breathe every day. We have to constantly inhale and exhale. We should look at that constant inflow and outflow of energy, and try to apply that to all areas, including physical exercise. That's why we have to sleep, so our body can rest and many internal repairs can be done at night. When we're up, we should be active; when we go to sleep, we should go to sleep and let those automatic functions of the body be taken care of by the appropriate parts of the mind-body complex.

Mental Exercise

The fourth element is mental exercise. *Always remember to balance the mind and body*. Our minds as well as our bodies get locked into rigid patterns. One of nature's laws is everything changes and if we don't acknowledge that, it's harder for us to function. The Chinese stress understanding change. We make assumptions about things being the same or people being the same and yet we change, we grow. We go through different stages and what we thought was foolish twenty years ago is important now and something we thought was important ten years ago is no longer important now. The Chinese say that if we allow our bodies to only work in certain rigid patterns, then when we suddenly have to do something else, we have problems because our bodies will not respond and function properly. It's the same with our minds. If we allow our minds to get into rigid patterns and then we have to cope with a sudden emergency, we get stuck, we're not able to respond. The idea is to keep the mind flexible, as well as the body.

For instance, look at a conflict from your perspective and the other person's and go back and forth between the two. See where the balance and harmony is between the two points. We're not always right, sometimes we're wrong, and more often than not, it's a little of both. There is a place of harmony and the place of harmony is the place of truth and honesty, where you accurately look at a situation in order to effectively change it. Not just to change for change's sake, but to look and see that sometimes we're correct in our appraisal, and many times we're inaccurate. Our vision of things is colored by emotion, feelings, and cultural assumptions that are not necessarily true; it's colored by ego, by what we've been taught by people who perhaps didn't know what they were talking about. Many of our mental patterns come from books. How do we know that the people who wrote the books knew what they were talking about?

When I started my acupuncture training with Master George Long, I asked him what books I should read, having been a scholar much of my life. He said, "Don't read any books; they'll just confuse you." It was hard, but I didn't read for awhile. And then, when I finally did read the books, I understood what he meant. When it comes to certain aspects of healing there are contradictory *opinions* expressed in books, some are even diametrically opposed. If you read the books before you have the practical experience, you'll say, "Well, this obviously is no good — how can this pulse diagnosis work when one person says it's this way and another person says it's that way?" But by the time I read the books, I had had real experience of pulse diagnosis, and knew what worked. Some of the people who write books don't know what they're talking about. Their knowledge is in their heads, not in their hands or their bodies, not in their lives. But someone who only operates from their head and thinks that's their center can become confused because from a head perspective all these different opinions and systems of thought seem valid. When you have the experience, though, it's a different matter. When you know, you know. Imagine a clear glass on a table, and sitting around the table with you are famous people from history — Albert

Einstein, Albert Schweitzer, and all the great physicians and metaphysicians. They all look at a clear glass and one says, "Well, obviously it's a glass of cold water." Another says, "No, obviously, it's a glass of warm water." And someone else says, "Ah, no, no, it's a glass of — it's a glass of vodka." Someone else says, "No, no, no, it's gin." So they argue about it, and while they're arguing, you reach over and pick up the glass and you taste the contents and it's a glass of warm water. As you set the glass down, Albert Einstein comes over and says, "Believe me, I know this is a glass of gin." You say, "Sorry, Al, it's not." "What do you mean?" he asks. "How do you know?" You say, "Because I tried it. While you guys were arguing, I tasted it." And that's the approach we need to take with these principles of Oriental medicine. Taste it. Experiment with it. We need to exercise our minds and our bodies to get them to work together.

Mental exercise is what I call bare awareness. Most people aren't there. I mean, we're not where we are. The Firesign Theater used to say, "How can you be in two places at once if you're not anywhere at all?" We're either in the past or in the future. We're not here and now. One of the first things I do with patients is get them to see what's really going on. Someone comes in and says, "I've got this terrible problem and I don't know why. Where did it come from? Who did this?" What they need to acknowledge is: "I did this. I put this here. I accept responsibility for putting this here." But I find that our culture has made it very easy for people to blame their illnesses on somebody or something out there. The germs did it. Something out there did it.

The Chinese don't really believe in the germ theory. There are germs around us all the time, but we're not sick all the time. Why not? Because our bodies have an immune system. If we get sick it means that on some level or another, our defense system has weakened. Essentially we're like a castle and in order for those invaders to get into the castle, somebody had to let the

80

drawbridge down and it doesn't happen from the outside, it happens from the inside. We weaken ourselves when we over-exert or we under-exercise, whenever we get into extremes. One of the first exercises I do with patients has to do with awareness. For example, I knew a woman who developed selective amnesia. Everytime the little light went on in the refrigerator, her consciousness went off. She would shut off her awareness and would not remember eating anything at all. Consequently, she couldn't understand why she continued to gain weight. Part of the solution is getting yourself to become aware of what's going on. Your body tells you what's going on all the time. It tells you, "Don't eat that." But we don't listen to it and if you don't listen often enough, then it stops talking to you. It says, "No more advice for you." We lose our inner guidance.

I think a good word to describe much of Oriental medicine and health care is *reasonableness,* being sensible. One thing I've discovered throughout the years is that *common sense is not very common* and that's really what good health care is. It's not a lot of complex rules. It's learning to listen to your body and be sensible about what you do to it and with it.

Case Histories: Specific Activities and Occupations

Case Histories:
Specific Activities and Occupations

In the course of my practice I have noted common health problems to be associated with particular occupations and activities. Auricular Acupuncture has been effective in treating these problems when combined with the patients' understanding of the factors creating the problem. The purpose of the following section is to illustrate the actions and conditions which contribute to these health problems.

Carpenters and Mechanics

These two occupations consistently provide people with lower back pain. There's an old saying, "As above, so below," and this applies to the spine. Damage to the lower back sets off a chain reaction which results in a corresponding cervical problem. This cervical pressure often results in headaches. Carpenters are constantly lifting and bending over and hammering in awkward positions and many times doing things their bodies are not prepared for, consequently, the lower back is over-used or abused. A person can become accustomed to doing physical exercise, but all it takes is one moment of non-awareness to pick something up the wrong way and overstress part of the body. All preventative techniques consider the body as a whole unit. Avoiding unnecessary stress or strain on any one part of the body is extremely important.

Mechanics are constantly bending over the fenders of cars and this puts a strain on the lower back. Being underneath cars and holding their arms up, and working with their arms up over long periods of time puts strain on the neck and shoulder area and this creates chronic tension and often chronic headaches. The value of acupuncture is it helps stimulate the body to repair itself and in these cases to interrupt the negative chain of reaction. The needles direct the flow of the body's energy to relax muscle spasms that cause pinched nerves in the lower back and cervical area.

Clerical Workers

First, on a physical level, most people who work in offices are either sitting down all day at typewriters or bending over files or are on their feet quite a bit. Sitting down and typing puts a tremendous strain on the neck and shoulder area and also the lower back. Most chairs are not properly designed to support the human body. Besides, it's not natural to have to sit for eight hours a day. I work with many people who do office work and have lower neck problems and back and shoulder problems, which can escalate into chronic headaches if worsened by the pressures and strains inherent in most jobs. One of the ways I work with these people is to teach them exercises which they can do to relieve the tension that builds up during the day and to get a better sense of their bodies and how they work so their systems can become more relaxed. The more relaxed your muscles are, the more capable they are of acting properly and not retaining unnecessary tension. If tension builds up it creates neck and shoulder problems and headaches. Clerical workers also tend to have lower back problems which often grow into sciatic problems, pinched nerves and poor circulation in the legs.

The second group of office workers I have observed are executives and people in positions of authority. Clerical workers deal with tension created by others, but executives often create their own tension. There's a lot of tension in most aspects of business. In this country many more men than women die of heart attacks and they die at earlier ages then women. One of the reasons for this is work connected stress. It also has to do with living in a male dominated culture with distorted ideas about masculinity. People become over-achievers, work too hard at some things and don't work at other things at all — people over-develop in certain systems and under-develop in others.

People live their lives without knowing how to relax. I spend a lot of time working with people just to get them to understand a little bit about relaxation because the basic approach of many people is, "OK, I don't know how to relax. I'm going to force myself to relax. I'm going to relax right now!" You can't do that. Relaxation is letting go, it's not grabbing onto something. The more you *try* to relax, the less likely you are to do it because you're trying to *force* something that has to occur naturally. Both executives and clerical workers in offices need a better understanding of relaxation. Many executives end up with hypertension, high blood pressure, and ulcers. They end up with conditions directly connected to stress. An ulcer is a good example of the importance of working with both the mind and the body. Ulcers don't just drop out of the sky. They're created by how we deal with stress and tension. They're created by what we eat and when we eat, and how we eat. If someone came to me with an ulcer, I could just stick the needles in the ear and not talk to him or her and the body would repair itself. But the chances are within six to nine months or even less, they'd have another ulcer simply because the mind must be involved in the process of undoing the problem just as the mind is involved in the making of the problem. If you wanted to untie a bundle of knots, you would have to untie the last knot first and then trace your way back to the first knot. The same with the body. It's like peeling an onion — retracing a pattern of growth. The last thing to go is the first to appear. The needles go directly to work on the physical body in dealing with ulcers and hypertension, and the dialogue that goes on during treatment has to do with the conditons that created the ulcer or the hypertension, how to repair the damage and how not to create these conditions in the future.

Domestic Engineers

I think this is a much better term than "housewives" which has developed a lot of negative overtones. The woman who stays home and takes care of children or the man who stays home and takes care of children, has to do an incredible number of difficult tasks on a day to day basis, and quite a variety of tasks requiring strength, subtlety and skill on many levels. Picking up children is one way many people hurt their backs. Lifting babies and carrying babies until they fall asleep puts strain on the arms, neck and shoulders. One of the common complaints of home-makers is headaches. There are many stresses and tensions when you're alone with children and have other obligations. A person often ends up putting all their energy out for others, for the children, for the home, for the husband, and this connects with patients who give all their energy to other people and therefore don't have enough for their own sustenance. In the house there are other occupational hazards. There's stress and tension because, again, in a male dominated culture there is a lack of value placed on things done at home. There have been instances where men and women exchange roles and the men find quickly they can't handle the job of home-maker or they have to make major adjustments in order to adapt to the range and variety of tasks they're required to do. At home, it's not just dealing with pieces of paper and formulas, it's dealing with living beings. When we're dealing with little children we're often dealing with people who can't communicate their problem, so *we* have to figure it out. As they get older and more verbal, we have to *work* to develop a way to understand how much freedom to give a child without crushing their spirit. On the other hand, how do we keep them from ruling our lives by having no restrictions? There are constant balancings in the process of effectively managing a family and a home.

Professional Athletes

Professional athletes are quite responsive to acupuncture. They're more knowledgeable about their bodies because their bodies are their profession. I've worked with athletes because in the martial arts and in professional sports, the knees are exceedingly vulnerable, but it's also an area in which acupuncture has been especially effective. Professional athletes from different fields (baseball, football, basketball, soccer) came to my teacher's clinic because the acupuncture would focus the body's energy on the knees and stimulate the body to repair itself and they were able to avoid operations and medication. Professional sports people were among the best patients because they knew about their bodies, they understood their bodies and were perceptive about the changes that occured in their bodies. They knew when their knees were better. They *knew* when they were able to lift heavier weights or do more exercises. They had many objective criteria by which they could gauge the effectiveness of the treatments. Professional athletes are excellent patients who get excellent results from properly administered acupuncture.

Artists and Musicians

People in the arts have special gifts and special problems because they are in public situations. They tend to manifest a lot of energy when they're performing, but are not necessarily able to maintain it when they're not. This relates to an application of balance. We need balance within the microcosm and in

89

the relationship between the microcosm and the macrocosm. In the Bay Area, I found acupuncture appropriate for performers who either had a recording session, an audition, or an important performance coming up. They would become overloaded with nervous energy prior to the time of their performance. The treatment would help them redistribute their energy, thereby balancing it more effectively so they could perform better. Any athlete, entertainer, or artist will tell you they function more effectively when relaxed, not relaxed in the sense of falling asleep or being limp, but relaxed in the sense of being able to tap into all their capabilities, all their potential, by not becoming locked into one area. That's what play really means to me. Play being being able to cover the range, to skip around and move and experiment and explore the endless possibilities that are presented to us when we escape from our own self-imposed belief systems, even momentarily. An artist spends years and years learning the art and technique of music, painting or writing. Then they may spend some time getting away from technique in order to get back in touch with their creativity. Artists need to balance work and play in their lives and my dialogue with them during treatment has to do with gaining a perspective on this balance.

What makes the artist available to us is a combination of technical skills and creative, spontaneous inspiration. There are, as someone said, a million mute insensate Wordsworths, people who feel the same things Wordsworth did, but lack the skills of expression. The skills must be developed through work, through applied effort. It's not the work that makes the artist, though without work there is not great art. It's a paradox, constantly we find paradox. But paradox is not something which doesn't make logical sense. Paradox is the essence of our nature. Opposing principles don't cancel each other out but rather allow us to experience the joy and vitality of life. There are people who work all the time on technique and never relax enough to let creativity flow, never relax enough to let themselves be spontaneous. Consequently, they remain masters of technique but never masters in the true sense of creative artists. There are other people who have tremendous surges of creativity, but don't have a technique through which to channel it, so their creativity evaporates. We need to have something to say on the inside and a way to say it on the outside. We need a balance of the left hemisphere and the right hemisphere, each doing their job, and the two working together.

Therapists

One of the themes you've probably noticed repeating over and over in these pages has been the concept of balance, both internal and external. One of the major balances is between mind and body. In the area of the "helping professions," the mind-body balance is delicate. Having worked with a number of professional therapists, I noticed a tendency toward what I call "light-switch thinking" or "push pull thinking." Some therapists tend to be either The Father or The Mother. The Father is all-wise and knowing and gives energy, information and knowledge to his patients. It's a pushing, forceful system. The Mother is more emotional, accepting the patient in whatever condition they are, absorbing the patient's negative energy, taking it all into themselves.

These systems aren't the way reality operates and eventually The Mother and The Father run into problems. For example, if you're giving energy all the time, you have to replenish it. If you don't know (or lose contact with) the methods of replenishing energy, then you're going to be forced to put out what you don't have and that's a problem. On the other hand, you can only absorb so much garbage (because you have your own garbage to process as well) before you run out of places to store it. What happened with many therapists that I saw was they got hooked into *one* of those modes and didn't replenish or recycle their energy. I look at the healing arts as a dialectical alchemical process. It's a back and forth process. I don't just take information from my patients, I process it and send it back to them and we gradually work at a process of purification, the result of which is both of us are better. You see, if you work it like a battery, where I'm a highly charged battery and someone comes in when their battery is dead, and hooks up and I give them energy, that's not good because that means they're still going to run down their battery and need to get charged again. But if we work it as an energy exchange where we both get vitalized by the process, then that person *learns* the process of vitalization himself or herself and isn't dependent on me for it. Also, I'm not drained at the end of the day because what good is it to be in the helping professions getting others to feel well, if it messes up your own life? There's something out of balance in that case. The same with the person who absorbs negativity from other people. People have to learn to process their own negative energy. Chogyam Trungpa, in one of his books, referred to our negative emotions and negative energy and all the garbage in our lives as compost. I think that's a great way to look at it, that it's something that would be distasteful if placed on the dinner table, however it has a certain purpose and function in the process of growth. Part of this push-pull system comes from being too much in the head and not enough in the body. One example is a professional therapist who came to me and among other things was slightly overweight. At one point, in inquiring what forms of exercise she did, I was told she loved walking. On further inquiry, I was told she actually didn't do any walking. So, I said, "Look, we have to be clear about how we use our words to describe reality. You may love *thinking* about walking, and you may love *talking* about walking, but if you *loved* walking, you'd walk." You have to be clear with youself about what you're doing. Many people I work with have a tremendous amount of information in their heads but they don't have it in their bodies. They don't use it. They don't apply it. We outsmart ourselves by thinking that if we understand something in our head, we know it. *Knowing* is a much more complete experience than mere intellectual appreciation. Many times we make that mistake in the area of body-knowledge by assuming and processing body knowledge through the intellect. Body knowledge is body knowledge.

Mind knowledge is mind knowledge. If each one does their job, then things are going well. But if they start doing each other's job, we run into problems. It's not often that someone attempts to process all their intellectual knowledge through their body, but it's more common in our culture for people to be top-heavy and attempt to process all body knowledge through their head. For example, I work with people on whatever levels they need to work, including that of physical exercise. Through the years I've learned various and sundry martial arts and healing arts and thousands of different exercises. If someone expresses a need to work on a certain part of the body, I will teach them specific exercises for their particular conditions. But what happens many times is that people do the exercises for a day or two and think, "Well, now that I know that, I don't need to do it anymore." And they don't do it anymore. They have it stored somewhere in their head. But the exercise is for the body. It doesn't do the head any good. Exercise for the body is to be done by the body. Then the people wonder why they didn't get as good results as the people who took the body exercises and *used* them for the body, and took the head exercises and used them for the head.

The kind of results I like to see are people knowing more about themselves, knowing how to maintain their own health, how to detect things before they get too far out of balance, and how to bounce back when they do get out of balance. Also, I love it when people can take the information which they have learned and pass it on to other people. To me that's a wonderful feeling. There have been times when I have met people for the first time, but through someone I treated several years ago they learned an effective way to deal with some health problem. And I wasn't even involved! I like that. I like to see that because there's an old Chinese saying that if you give a man a fish, you feed him for a day, but if you teach a man to fish, you feed him for life. Give people a skill they can use and apply themselves rather than making them dependent on someone else.

Female Complaints

I don't like that title very much, though I haven't come up with a more effective one. This section concerns problems women have, and especially women in the West. There are many reasons for this. The first, of course, is that this is a male dominated culture, which means there is less accurate information about women and a less accurate expression of the nature of woman in society. I have worked with many women who had a poor understanding of their own cycles and rhythms, and this was partly because of not having accurate information available to them through the literature of our culture. The menstrual cycle is a complex and wondrous process. It's a process that is examined in the West primarily from a physiological standpoint and, as we've said before, nothing is totally physical or totally mental or totally emotional. There's always a combination, there's always an overlap and an interface. To look at any phenomena from a purely physical standpoint would be to take a simplistic view which will lead eventually to confusion and a lack of understanding and, therefore, disharmony.

The emotional component of the menstrual cycle and menopause is often overlooked or treated in a simplistic fashion. To me emotions are important because they perform a function similar to that of the corpus collosum which connects the left and right hemispheres of the brain. Emotions connect mind and body. You can start out thinking about something or a situation in the mind, and through the wonder of emotions, experience physiological sensations. On the other hand, you can experience certain physiological sensations, and when you connect them with an emotion, you will connect them with a person or situation. The emotions act as a bridge between mind and body, the intellectual and the physical. This is an extremely important factor in looking at the process of the menstrual cycle, pregnancy, childbirth and menopause. In each one of them there are physiological substances being released which trigger both physical and emotional reactions. These emotional reactions effect one's mental set, the way one feels about people and events. If this isn't taken into consideration, many actions appear nonsensical or irrational. However, if you begin to understand the complexities of your system, then it's easier to follow what's going on. One of the problems that acupuncture is successful with is irregular menstrual cycles and other abnormalities of the menstrual cycle. The reason is the needles send a message to the brain, the brain interprets that message and then acts to regulate the body, and restore the natural state of health and harmony. The message of the needles is repeated until the body is doing the rebalancing on its own without the need of further stimulation.

In dealing with menstrual difficulties, one of the most common problems has to do with women who were placed on birth control pills at an early age in order to regulate their cycle. What happens is, no matter how good the chemical substance is, it still is a foreign substance in the body, which means the body has to process and deal with the side effects (which are not necessarily positive) of the chemical. The second factor is the body becomes trained to recognize what is essentially a false signal, and so in the case of birth control pills, the body is getting an internal neuro-chemical, hormonal message to ovulate and then in comes a very powerful (but obviously foreign) chemical message telling the body not to ovulate. There's an internal conflict. But the chemical message is so powerful, it overpowers the natural messages. The body starts paying attention to the chemical message, ignoring the natural message. This sets up a disharmony, a dysfunction. It's as if a stranger comes into your house, and you believe the stranger but not a member of your own family. So the member of your family will stop sending you messages. Then the stranger goes away, i.e., you stop taking the birth control pills. You find out they're doing things that are not good for you or there are side effects. So you stop taking them. Well, that family member may be reticent to talk to you again because you've been ignoring their messages for a long time. Maybe they'll stop sending you messages. Even if they send you messages again, you may be so used to recognizing the foreign signals that you continue to ignore the natural signals. There has to be a period of reconditioning. There has to be a sort of shock or jolt to get the body to begin to recognize its own signals instead of looking for a foreign message that is very powerful. Many women go three, four, five, up to six months or more without having a period. This creates tension in the body, emotional and mental tension, which creates disharmony. Acupuncture works with getting the body to begin to recognize its own signals, accept its own internal messages as valid, and to follow those messages rather than wait for an external and foreign signal. It stimulates the body back to its natural state of health and balance.

Acupuncture can be effective in pregnancy and childbirth. Recently we had a son born to us at home with a midwife and doctor present, and things went smoothly and naturally. One factor was the preparation we did beforehand. My wife prepared for childbirth as if for an athletic event. She drank three to four quarts of water a day to keep her system clean. She watched her diet and ate things which were good for her body. She exercised daily. She did Tai Chi Chuan up until a month before the baby was born and exercised mentally by doing self-hypnosis, relaxation techniques and visualization to prepare for the birth process. We worked together to prepare and the birth went smoothly. In another case I assisted in delivering a baby through acupuncture by treating the mother who had been in labor for fifteen hours without properly dilating. After treating her, she relaxed and fell asleep. Later she woke and went into a smooth, natural labor without having to consider the possibility of a Caesarean section. The body has a wisdom of its own, and if the individual works with, supports and learns from that body-wisdom, the body will do its job properly.

The third area involves menopause, which is, again, another major change in the system. Remember? The essential nature of reality, the one thing that *doesn't change,* is that *everything changes.* We have to understand this not only intellectually but emotionally, and physiologically. Our bodies change, and we should not try and hold onto the previous stage, but move into the next stage as smoothly and successfully as possible. One of the bizarre things about Western culture is the extreme, unhealthy emphasis on youth. Youth is a part of the life-process, but trying to regain lost youth is an extreme sort of folly. We're all going to die. We can't avoid it and there's nothing wrong with that. That's part of the process. That's one of the things we have to deal with in a reasonable fashion, and avoiding it and trying to go backwards in time is not the way to be reasonable. We should enjoy each phase of the process of being alive for what it is, rather than wanting it to be something else. I believe that if a person maintains their health — mental, physical, emotional, spiritual — they will have a vitality that will often be interpreted as youthfulness and vivacity regardless of their chronological age. Almost everyone, during treatment, gets back in touch with their own vitality. People will comment on this change, saying, "Gee, you look different. What have you been doing?" But it's a vitality that comes from the *inside out* and has to do with being in touch with one's own connection to the source of all energy and vitality. Getting back to the subject of menopause: this is another change in the menstrual cycle. If people aren't prepared for it, or if people are afraid of it, because it represents being one step closer to dying, then a dissonance is set up in the body, a disharmony, an imbalance. This imbalance will cause certain systems to shut down, will cause energy to be unbalanced by shifting too much energy to some places and not enough energy to others. Hot flashes and various other symptoms indicate the process of change is occurring. But if that process isn't accepted and incorporated into one's existence on a mental, physical and emotional level, then there will be stress, dissonance and imbalance.

Questions and Answers

Questions and Answers

Question: *Are there any acupuncture points in the ear and can ear piercing have any effect on them?*

There are over two hundred points in the external ear that are used in auricular acupuncture. Relatively few points are on the lobe. Generally when people get their ears pierced it's in the eye point. If the body keeps getting a constant signal from any one point and there's nothing wrong with that area, it disregards it after a period of time, so it really doesn't matter. If you stimulate a point with the needles, the body sends a neurological message to the brain and the brain interprets that message, and says, "OK, we'll send a crew down there." And the crew says, "It's OK, it's an earring," and they cancel the message. So, ear piercing doesn't do any harm.

Question: *How do you feel about using acupuncture to help me stop smoking?*

It's fairly easy to stop smoking once you make your internal decision to quit. I can't work with someone if they're double binding — "I really want to quit; no, I don't." If someone doesn't want to quit, they fight a battle inside themselves. If they make that internal decision, acupuncture focuses the

101

body's energy more effectively. It focuses energy on the lungs so they recuperate in 1/3 the time it normally takes. Acupuncture is also used to focus on the problem of too much energy in one place. If you quit smoking, you've got a lot of nervous energy and if you don't do something with it, it goes into the next available automatic process — eating. You don't want that. You don't want to start eating more because you're not smoking. The idea is to work with distributing energy more effectively. I've had good results with people who really want to quit and I'm selective about whom I treat. I don't want to waste anybody's time or money and I don't want to waste my time either.

No one was born smoking. You have to learn what brand to get and how to open the pack, which hand to hold the cigarette in, what kind of lighter to use, your style. And once you learn that, it becomes automatic. You can practically do it in your sleep. Therefore, when you want to quit smoking, you have to send an observer down to the subconscious to look at the process of smoking and make all those automatic actions conscious. That's where bare awareness or attention comes in. I instruct people to pay attention to when they smoke, how they smoke, and what they're doing while they smoke. I used to smoke three packs of Pall Malls a day; that's sixty cigarettes daily. At one point I realized, "Hey, I don't think I'm really enjoying this." I tried to quit a number of times and failed. I started looking at how many cigarettes I really enjoyed and found I only *remembered* about ten of them. The rest were consumed automatically. I'd look in the ashtray and see another two butts, and I'd say, "Who did that?" It was me. The first thing I had to do was make my unconscious behavior conscious and then I was able to pick up, "Oh, I did that. And I'm about to light another one!" You can't kid yourself *all* the time. If you start really paying attention to what you're doing, if you start being aware, you can't get away with that stuff very long. For example, I knew one woman who wanted to quit smoking. She made the decision to quit and didn't have any cigarettes for three days. Then she came in as if she'd done something bad. She'd had a cigarette. I said, "OK, avoid light-switch thinking, it's not all off or all on. You went three days without a cigarette. You had one cigarette in four days. That's much better than two packs every day." I asked her, "Where did that cigarette come from?" "Oh, the drawer in the living room," she answered. "Well, your husband doesn't smoke, does he?" I asked. "No." I asked her how she happened to have the cigarettes in the drawer. "Oh, I have them around," she answered. She was saying, "Yes, I really want to quit, but I don't dare quit." We've got to analyze every detail to get habituated to clear thinking about our actions. We say, "It happened so fast, I didn't have time to think about it." Well, we have to *take time to think*. She not only had cigarettes there, she had matches. She had an ashtray. So I said, "OK, I want you to put the ashtray on one side of the room and the matches on the other side, and I want you to think about it when you get the matches. Think about what you're doing. Ask yourself, am I a smoker or a non-smoker?"

She came back the next day and said, "I can't do it. I can't do it. I can't fool myself anymore. It takes too long to walk across the living room and by the time I'm halfway there, I know what I'm doing." The simple technique of putting a little time element between her impulse and her action became so complex, she couldn't make any more excuses. If you apply the principles of awareness to one thing, you can apply them to everything.

Question: *Do you work with dieting? I had a friend once who went to an acupuncturist and had something put in her ear and whenever she touched it, she wasn't hungry anymore.*

Sometimes I do work with people who need to lose weight, but I'll only do it if it's really a serious, health impairing problem. I use a small needle called a press needle that looks like a tiny thumb tack. It's used between regular treatments to augment a program of treatments combined with patient awareness and involvement. I screen out many people over the phone, especially those who are looking for some magic pill or one session or something that's going to do it *for them* so they can continue eating all the things they want. Many people don't want to participate in the process. You have to *participate* and you have to *do* things if you really want to make changes in your system. Weight is one of the hardest things to deal with because a person has to get involved with working on it themselves. Once you quit smoking you don't need to think about smoking again. But you can't say, "Hey, I just had a great meal. I ate it quite well. Now I don't have to worry about eating again." You have to keep eating. It's easy for us to do light-switch thinking, all on or all off. Either I'm going to smoke or I'm a non-smoker. But it's hard to say, "Well, I'd like to change my eating habits a little. I'11 have to watch my breathing a little. I'11 have to exercise a little more and I'11 have to use my awareness of eating, exercising and breathing a little more." That's harder, making slight changes. But those slight changes can have lasting results.

Question: *How can acupuncture help me with beauty and skin care?*

The Chinese felt it was a mistake to change things from the outside when you weren't working on change from the inside. If you feel good on the inside, if all your organs are doing their job and you feel healthy, it shows. The Chinese say your skin is your third lung. It's another way your body breathes. In new Western medical textbooks, they actually list skin as an organ. It's an organ of respiration and an organ of elimination. If certain internal organs aren't doing their job eliminating, it affects your skin. Your body eliminates through your intestines and your kidney-bladder system. Your liver processes toxins out of your system. Your breath actually contains waste materials. Certain things your body can't process are released through your breath and through your skin. Perspiration is your pores opening and releasing toxins and waste materials. Many skin problems reflect something inside that's not working properly. Acupuncture is a way to stimulate the body to repair the things inside and then it reflects on the outside. I've worked with a number of people who have dermatology problems. Either the problem is with the lungs, the kidney-bladder system, or the liver and it's processing of toxins. Oriental medicine works on the internal organs and when they are healthy, it reflects on the outside. I've gotten good results with so-called "incurable" skin ailments. In one case the person had a bad liver which was not processing toxins. The liver was saying, "I can't filter this stuff. Send it to the skin!" So that person had a skin problem. With other people it was the kidney-bladder system that wasn't working properly. That's fairly common in this culture. I could talk for hours on just kidney-bladder problems because coffee, alcohol, and drinks with sugar tend to overwork and damage the kidney-bladder system.

Question: *How do you deal with allergies and asthma?*

Allergies and asthma are extreme reactions in the body. Whenever pollens are released, everyone's body reacts and adjusts. But some people have severe over-reactions. Acupuncture stimulates the body's ability to heal itself. The body's core is well balanced and when atuned to the environment will not over-react. For example, people with certain skin problems have over-sensitive skin. If your skin wasn't sensitive at all, you could hurt yourself and not know it. If your skin was too sensitive, the air would hurt! There is a place of balance between the two extremes. It's similar with allergies and asthma.

Recently three patients came in before the allergy season. I was able to treat them preventively to strengthen their systems before everything was released into the air. Other allergy prone people around them were sneezing, but these three were doing much better, except one who lets his head control his body too much. This person would say, "Yeah, the first breath of pollen comes around, I just sneeze once and, ah, there it goes again." He's like an all day radio station playing tapes. "Here's the old asthma tape, I'm just going to plug it in." He was assuming, as soon as he sneezed once, his body would follow the old patterns. If I can interrupt negative assumptions, maybe people can see that there are other possibilities. People have headaches and when they start, they say, "Oh, no, here comes another one." So the body says, "OK, let's play, 'Oh, God, headache number 404.'" And it repeats, the same old pattern, and every time it's repeated it becomes so automatic that little prodding is needed to get the tape moving.

Question: *What is the difference between acupressure and acupuncture and do the points on one side of the body correspond to the points on the other side of the body? If you work on one point, does it effect that same point on the other side of the body?*

Acupressure and acupuncture are based on the same system. Acupressure is more useful in a preventative, general maintenance way. Acupuncture is more specific and powerful and therefore works on many things which acupressure cannot necessarily influence.

The pressure point large intestine 4, is used for neck and shoulders. It's also used for headaches and for an analgesic for the throat area. It can be used on either side.

Question: *I found your comments on the flight or fight mechanism interesting. Could you explain more?*

The kidney-bladder system is damaged by over-stimulation of what's called the flight or fight mechanism. When people are at work and they get angry or upset, it stimulates a very primitive mechanism. The adrenal gland that sits on top of the kidney produces adrenalin because if you're going to punch somebody or you're going to run away, you want energy. But, in our culture and in work and social situations, we don't punch and we don't run. We say, "Oh, yes sir." And we absorb it. Scientific studies show that adrenalin that isn't processed, that isn't burnt off, can damage muscle tissue. The fight or flight mechanism also sends a message to empty the bladder because if you want to run, you need an empty bladder. If you want to fight, you need an empty bladder. The message goes down for the bladder to evacuate, and the mind says, "No, don't you dare!" That's not socially acceptable. So we send, through the conscious mind, a contradictory message to cancel the order. As a result, the body gets the natural signal on one side and another signal, to countermand that order, on the other side, and at the same time it's loaded with adrenalin. This puts stress on the kidney-bladder system. The bladder gets mixed signals: "Well, I guess we should — no, maybe — well, I guess we should — no." And it's almost a schizoid process. That's because we haven't learned ways to deal with stress situations other than activating that primitive system and repressing it. The value of Tai Chi Chuan and martial arts exercises and other breathing exercises is to train you to breathe better, and calm down to deal with stress. One of the real values of Chinese health practices is they teach you how to cope with situations. We can make things worse by the way we react to them. For example, a dog growls at you. You become upset and afraid. The dog knows this from your body language. Because a dog's hearing is twelve to thirteen times more sensitive than a human being's he can also hear your breath becoming rapid and shallow, and that tells him you're afraid. Also, part of that message to evacuate when you're afraid causes you to sweat, and your sweat releases the smell of adrenalin. Then the dog knows he's got you. These factors make the dog bold enough to confront you because he knows on at least three levels that you're afraid. Oriental practices teach you to deal with fear. Essentially there's one fear: fear of death. When we learn to deal with, accept and understand that, then we can deal with a lot of little piddly stuff during the day without getting upset. It goes back to understanding the nature of reality as change and that means as soon as we're born, the one thing we know is that we're going to die. It's the other side of the coin. It's nothing to be upset about because it's going to happen to all of us. The point is to enjoy our lives in between. Many people are so afraid of dying, they never live. The fear of death that's never really dealt with comes out in the form of fear in general. If you look in a medical dictionary you'll see several pages of phobias and if you really trace them back, they're all, in one way or another, connected with the fear of dying. But here's the advantage — if you learn to deal with that basic one, the rest will clear up.

Question: *What about eye problems?*

Acupuncture is a scientific, systematic way to stimulate the body to repair itself. Many types of eye problems have been treated in China: glaucoma, cataracts, and other eye conditions. The body retains it's basic ability to repair itself and it is stimulated by acupuncture. Success depends on an accurate diagnosis, the general energy level of the person, and their willingness to participate. There's one big difference between Eastern and Western medicine: I never heal anyone 100%. I do 80%. The patient has to do 20%. You have to participate in the process to know it was your body that did it. Instead of people leaving thinking I've corrected their problem, I want people to leave knowing their own mind-body system *corrected itself.* I've treated things that were supposedly incurable and people got excellent results. Then I sent them for medical testing and they came back from their doctors with one of two comments: "Well, that's a coincidence," or, "Spontaneous remission." I thought about changing the name of what I do to Coincidental Spontaneous Remission. But I really don't care about the name, I care about results. Results come from a combination of what acupuncture does and what the person does. It's those five elements I spoke of previously. It's getting people involved in their health instead of them saying, "I don't need to know anything about my body because 'they'll' take care of it.'' What if 'they're' not there? I don't look at being responsible for my health as a burden. I appreciate having more power over myself instead of being dependent on someone or something out there to take care of me. I like being independent in that sense. I like understanding how my body works because it helps me to avoid doing things that upset it too much. Many times we're our own worst enemy. There's a little voice that says, "You really shouldn't have that chocolate eclair you know," yet we go ahead and have it. Then we have an allergic reaction or a headache or upset stomach or we gain two pounds because we didn't listen to our bodies. I believe the feeling of being healthy is well worth the time and energy it takes to regain control of your system.

Question: *What if they don't find anything physiologically wrong with your body but your mind's all messed up? What can you do then? Anything at all?*

One time in the Bay Area I was working with people who were mentally disturbed and I found that with everyone I worked with, there was either an undiagnosed physiological ailment or a misdiagnosed physiological ailment. I'll give you an example of a particular patient. The state had taken away her children because they said she was an unfit mother. When I started working with her I said one day that she looked like she was in pain and she told me she wasn't. I knew there was distress in her body from her pulses. It turned out she had physiological complaints nobody had acknowledged and they didn't show up on the x-rays or on any of her tests, so she was told it was all in her head. She had physical pain that nobody believed was real. What do you do if you have constant pain that nobody believes? You stop telling people about it, but that doesn't make it go away. It gets worse. It can make you irritable to be in pain all the time, especially if you have to be with small children. I diagnosed there was something wrong with her reproductive system. I told her to go back to the

109

hospital for a check-up. They had written her off as a mental case because nothing showed on her previous tests, but I told her to demand re-testing. They found one of her ovaries was severely inflamed. She came back and I treated her for that. She got better and it changed her mental attitude because someone had acknowledged her physiological problem and found it instead of saying it was all in her head. Many people have pain and are told it's their imagination. But pain is pain. I'll help anyone really interested in healing themselves of pain. I'll help them find where it comes from and how to get rid of it. Sometimes people find they don't want to get rid of their pain. They've grown accustomed to the accomodations it makes for them. I saw that happen to a man whose wife went to work while he was sick. He came for treatment and found he could be cured. He got upset because that meant he'd have to go back to work. He couldn't handle it so he stopped treatment.

Question: *How can I help myself become aware of my breathing?*

Every once in a while during the day, focus on the lower abdomen and take a couple of deep breaths. If you start tuning in to your breathing, your body will respond and after a while you will change your way of breathing. You will find yourself breathing in the lower abdomen more and you'll find it does make certain changes. While walking is a good time to check your breathing. You can develop a nice rhythm while walking of inhaling and exhaling, as long as where you walk there's good fresh air. Don't walk next to a line of traffic, breathing in car fumes.

Remember, everything has a balance. That means, when you inhale you let the abdominal muscles relax. When you exhale, you pull them in. This expansion-contraction makes your muscles healthy. Look at the mechanics of the body. If a muscle contracts on one side, that means one has to expand on the other side. You have extensors and flexors. For every movement

110

that you make there's a balance. One's Yin and one's Yang. The same applies to muscles in the abdominal area. They are flexible to expand and have the strength to contract. This massages everything inside the abdominal cavity and makes sure your lungs empty out.

Question: *I was wondering about electronic acupuncture.*

I use electrical stimulation in certain cases but only if nothing else works. I use the least amount of energy to do the job. I'm old fashioned. I like to use needles because I know they work. I don't use electrical stimulation very often. I prefer to let the body repair itself. You can operate on two levels: one is the way which will stimulate a person to take care of themselves, physically or mentally; or, you can give somebody something — you can give them your energy, like a battery charger. I don't like that because it doesn't necessarily stimulate your system to cope or repair. You just get some of my charge. Then I've got to go out and recharge, and you have to keep coming to me.

Question: *How long do the needles stay in?*

In Auricular Acupuncture, the needles remain in the ear for twenty to thirty minutes.

Question: *You mentioned endorphins. What are they?*

They're brain peptides. The first one to be observed was beta endorphin, by Dr. Wu, a Chinese endocrinologist-brain specialist who extracted it from the pituitary gland of camels. Science didn't know what to do with it or what it was for. More recently, research has revealed that they're brain substances, 200-400 times more powerful than morphine, which are released by *your* brain, by your body. They fit the same receptors that morphine does. They're incredibly powerful substances the body can release not just to kill pain but to alleviate the pain so the body can repair itself. That's one thing that has been very much misrepresented about acupuncture. It's commonly believed that acupuncture will only treat symptoms. It's not true. Acupuncture goes to the *cause* of the problem. For example, if there's a problem on the skin, there's a problem inside the body. It usually has to do with the lung or the liver or the kidneys. It has to do with the body's ability to eliminate. The skin is an organ; it's your third lung. It is another way your body breathes, a way your body releases toxins. So if there's any problem with the outside of your body, it means something is going on inside.

Question: *I had a question a while back on habits, about twitching habits, that sort of thing.*

Twitching is often a random firing of a muscle. The muscle does it because of too much energy stored in it. Energy can be looked at as electrical and twitching is a discharging of that energy. Too much energy is being stored, or too much tension.

Question: *Right now I have this habit of twitching in my jaw and it goes down into my neck, and I'll have twitching in my eye.*

You just hit on three of the chronic tension areas: the neck and shoulders, the jaw, and the eyes. As people become tense their shoulders rise. That contributes to tension headaches and poor circulation. As you tighten these muscles, the blood supply is cut off. The major veins and arteries for the hands and arms go through the shoulder area. If an arm is tense, it cuts down the flow of blood. If the flow of blood is cut down, the circulation is cut down. If the circulation is cut down, then the temperature is lowered. When the temperature is lowered you get cold hands — poor circulation in your hands. You can get arthritis as a result of that. It's important to know how to relieve tension in the neck and shoulders.

I teach my patients exercises for the relief of tension in the neck and shoulders but tension also involves patterns of dealing with stress. If your patterns are negative and unhealthy, you've got to learn new ones. You can learn how to get the tension out and you can learn how not to take it in. You can learn to be like a duck and let it roll off your back.

The second stress area is the jaw. In the process of doing massage, I learned that the areas most often overlooked are the feet, hands, face, and particularly the jaw. Why tension in the jaw? It's all those things you wanted to say and never said and you held back and bit your tongue and clamped your jaw shut and took them inside and stored them. You stored them in your mind *and* in your jaw.

From the audience: "Well, I let it all out last night and it should be better today."

But that's one night of letting it out. What about all those years of storing it up, even as children? There's a story about a child who was running around and running around and the mother finally said, "You sit over there in the corner" and the child sat and said, "OK, I'm sitting, but in my head I'm running around." We all do that in one form or another.

The third area for tension is the eyes. Again, we tend to over-value our heads. It's *so* important to have a good head on our shoulders. Our eyes are *so* important. We read and study and look at television and watch movies, and it's very important how we use our eyes. We create a lot of tension and strain in the muscles around our eyes, and when we use our eyes too much or improperly, we fatigue these muscles. We always have something to do with our eyes because we're an ocular culture, and we store tension in those muscles. When people get acupuncture treatments and relax, they often say, "Well, the colors seem brighter, the plants seem greener, and it seems like somebody turned the lights up." Their peripheral vision increases because when we're trying to do something, we force it. We force our eyes by staring at something, we cut down our range of vision. When we relax, our peripheral vision opens. In the martial arts, you have to use your total field of vision because if you stare too much at someone's hand or face, you can get hit by a foot that comes around the side. Similarly in driving. I drive with my eyes relaxed because I see more on the side that way. The eyes, the jaw and the shoulders are three prime tension areas. And tension that you don't release often says, "Oh, well, she won't release it, we'll do it for her." And so the muscles twitch.

Question: *I find myself gritting my teeth in my sleep, and I wake up and I'm like that.*

In some cases people who grit their teeth at night are trying to hold back the subconscious because they're used to holding back during the day.

Question: *Could you say something about Shiatsu?*

Shitatsu is a Japanese version of acupressure using fingers, knuckles, thumbs and elbows on the acupuncture points to rebalance the body. I think one of the values of these systems is the fact that they get people back into their bodies. We tend to be so much in our heads that the body can't keep up, and physical manipulation can help get you back in your body. The second thing about it is that it has to do with touch and nonverbal communication. I believe that most healing arts are effective, in one way or another, because they involve the laying on of hands, physical contact, touching someone so the person's body learns from your body and not just from your words. I think words are often superfluous. All of this head stuff is OK, but what's really important is the message a person's vitality gives you. You can go to someone who can tell you all the right things about quitting smoking but maybe their body is telling you that they smoke two packs a day. The body message is the carrier wave, the energy level is the carrier wave, and words just ride along on top of the waves. If there's dissonance in the waves, people will listen to the words and not respond to them. Lots of people write great books but the important thing is their experience rather than their words.

Question: *I just wondered what role Shiatsu could play, along with acupuncture.*

My theory is, the least amount of energy that does the job. If people can be relieved of their problem by being massaged, that's fine. Acupressure and Shiatsu are ways to work with a person's health on a daily, preventative basis, but for major health problems, the needles perform a vital function because of their strength, power and accuracy. Acupuncture is a *direct* and *specific* way to stimulate the mind-body's natural healing capacity.

Question: *What is Tai Chi?*

This is the Tai Chi diagram. Tai Chi means Supreme Ultimate. This represents the supreme ultimate diagram. If you understand this you understand anything. My Tai Chi Chuan teacher is, among other things, a professional photographer. He's also a stereo and hi-fi enthusiast. One day he explained Tai Chi in terms of a tone arm. If the principle is good you should be able to apply it anywhere. If it only works on abstract grounds then it's only an abstract principle, it's no good in life. So if it's a good one it should work anywhere. He realized that in checking for a good tone arm, it had to be balanced. If the tone arm is too heavy it will mark the record, it won't track right, it won't give appropriate sound and it won't produce sound when you want it to. If it's too light it will skip around and bounce. If it's a heavy arm it will only play a perfect record, whereas an arm that's just right will play any record because it will *follow*.

The same principle applies in health. It's the same principle of balance that applies in movement arts like Tai Chi Chuan. But Tai Chi Chuan is a martial art and what most of you have probably seen is very slow, a meditation in motion. It started out as a martial art. It's an excellent fighting art though what has become known in this country are the other aspects of it. It's a form of meditation, a good exercise and it's good for the circulation, but it started out as a fighting art. You work at developing balance, not just physical balance, but mental balance. When you're doing the exercise, you're doing it with mind and body united. It's not like you were doing something with your body and you were thinking, "What are we going to have for dinner? What movie will we see?"

It takes about a year to learn the form, depending on the style. I do what's called Wu style. Most people in this country teach Yang style. It takes about a year to learn the form and I studied with one teacher, and after I had just about finished a form, he said, "Oh, you've just about finished the form." "Yeah," I replied, jokingly, "I finished the form, now I've got twenty years to get it right." He leaned over and looked me up and down and said, "No, only about seven years." It's the kind of thing you work on and when you think you've really got it, you start all over, you become a beginner again. It's a holistic projection of the principles of balance and harmony. The body is divided into Yin and Yang, front and back, right and left. For example, in the first movement, the arms move, the upper half of the body moves, and when your arms stop, then the lower body moves and when the lower body stops, the upper body moves, and left and right, and then the arms stop, and then the upper body moves. There's always a balance going on and very seldom is the weight on both feet. That's being double-weighted, like trying to be in both places at once. For example, this kind of step forward is called an empty step because there's no weight on the front leg, and then the weight is shifted forward, and there's no weight on the back leg. The reason for that is very simple in the martial sense, if you're fighting, you don't want your opponent to know if there's any weight on your foot. If there's weight on the forward foot then when your opponent sweeps your foot, you'll fall down. You want the forward foot to be empty and if somebody tries to sweep you, it can be rapidly moved. You can't do that if there's weight on that foot because *in the time* it takes you to shift your weight back, you'll fall. Tai Chi Chuan is a physical exercise and a form of meditation and concentration too. You have to *be there*. You can't drift off. You have to focus on what you're doing. You've got to exercise your whole body.

Oriental medicine, and Tai Chi Chuan in particular, develops the mind and body in harmony. When you're doing exercises, you should be there doing the exercises instead of thinking about what you're going to do next or what you did before so that the mind and the body can work together. A lot of people do exercises, and if they've been doing them long enough, they don't think about them. They think about something else and leave the body all alone to do the exercises. The body doesn't like that.

Question: *How would Tai Chi work with physical exercises? I go three times a week and take physical exercises.*

The one thing about Tai Chi Chuan is that you have to make a commitment to set aside a certain amount of time to work on it every day. That's what gets results. With Tai Chi Chuan you put in a half hour or forty-five minutes a day. Nobody has any more hours in the day than anybody else and yet people accomplish varying amounts of things by how they use their time. I get people who say, "Well, I don't know. A half an hour, that's a lot of time." Then it's not for them.

A class meets once a week and the lesson is an hour and a half, but that is a concentrated hour and a half of focused work. Then the student works individually during the week because there's what you learn from your teacher and there's what you learn from yourself. The best thing any teacher can do is help you learn how to learn from your own body because that's the real secret.

Question: *Is there an age limit for doing Tai Chi Chuan?*

No, my patients go from age 7 to 87. No matter what your age, you have to pay attention to your body. There's a well-known Tai Chi Chuan master in Boston who had a heart attack, a stroke, when he was about forty-six and his health was bad in other aspects, so he went to another master and started to learn Tai Chi Chuan to get his health back. He's now over eighty and incredibly healthy. He teaches Tai Chi Chuan to other people and he spars with younger men and does quite well. Tai Chi Chuan is gentle, flowing and rhythmic and develops circular movements instead of rigid, angular movements. It's designed to keep you flexible. I've seen people start in their seventies because you can do it at whatever level your body is capable of, and you keep doing it, you just keep working at it. Gradually your body becomes stronger and more capable. You don't force yourself to do anything. Someone

118

who is seventeen years old can do it much more vigorously than someone who is thirty, and someone who is sixty does it a little less vigorously. Another age will do it at a different pace. But each will benefit their health. The most valuable thing in learning it is *consistency*. I'll often teach patients exercises, both mental and physical, which are appropriate to their condition. When I teach people things, it's the people who consistently do the exercises who get results because then they own it. Many times people do the exercises for a few days and remember it in their heads, then they stop doing it in their bodies. The physical exercise remembered isn't worth very much. It's not what's in your head, it's what you've learned in your body that counts. Five minutes every day is better than 30 minutes once in a while. If every morning when you got up and every night before you went to bed you sat down for five minutes and just relaxed, did deep breathing into the lower abdomen and counted your breaths, one two three . . . up to ten, then started at one again, you would see benefits within a month or less. Five minutes in the morning and five minutes at night. *Every day.* But you know what most people do? They say, "Oh, if five minutes is good, fifteen minutes is even better." So you do fifteen minutes one day and you don't do anything the next day, you do ten minutes the next day, and then you don't do it for three days. Then you say, "Well, I did twenty-five minutes, why didn't it work?" Consistency is doing a small amount regularly.

Question: *I have a friend who just came back from China and she said at 6:00 in the morning, everyone is on the street doing Tai Chi, young and old, everybody. They do it in the evening too. And you don't see any fat Chinese. You don't see any heavy Oriental people.*

Another reason the Chinese do not tend to be overweight has to do with balancing the elements in their diet. In China you don't sit down and eat 16 oz. Porterhouse steaks. When you have meat, it's in small amounts in relation to vegetables.

Additional Thoughts On . . .

Additional Thoughts On . . .

Water

Sometimes the things that trip us up are the simplest ones, little things that we take for granted, like water. Certain problems are made more complex by not drinking enough water. People who are concerned with weight control and have been told they retain water or feel they retain water try to compensate by not drinking it. Wrong thinking. Just the opposite of what you need to do. If you're not drinking enough water, the crew inside the body says, "We're not getting enough of this stuff. We better hang onto it." So it stores the water. Whereas if you're drinking plenty of water, the body says, "Hey, it's OK, just hose down the lungs with this and let it flush through. We get plenty of this stuff every day."

Drinking water is crucial to flush out not only the kidney-bladder system but also the lungs and skin. Many people's pores get clogged because of the things they eat and the way they eat and what they do or don't drink. We can go without water for long periods of time, but that doesn't mean we should unless we're doing it for a particular reason. Drinking water is one of those simple things that tend to get overlooked. People who have kidney trouble often make it worse by not drinking water, which keeps the system overloaded with toxins that don't get flushed out because drinking water is one way your body purifies and cleanses itself.

Sleep and Dreams

Another simple thing that often gets over-looked is sleep. People tend to look past the obvious things, past the every day sort of things and look for mysterious and abstract solutions to health problems and health questions.

But sleep is extremely important and it's another one of those Yin-Yang balances, not too little, not too much. It's also related to exercise — how much exercise we get will have an effect on how much sleep we need. If you get a lot of sleep and don't get exercise, you'll tend to need more sleep and still feel tired. Whereas if you exercise a little bit, you'll need less sleep. If you exercise even more, you'll need even less sleep. Some of the most active and vigorous people I know of never sleep more than four or five hours a night. These are people who exercise at least two or three hours every day and some of them are in their sixties and seventies. We don't necessarily need a lot of sleep. What we need is quality, not quantity. When we sleep the body does its repair work and recharges itself. It's important that we get the *depth* of sleep needed and part of that relates to how effectively we're discharging our tension during the day. If we're not coping with things, if we're merely suppressing them rather than dealing with them during the day, then we carry that tension into sleep. Either we don't get deep enough to dream because as we relax those things we suppressed tend to float towards the surface, or we do have dreams which give us bizarre interpretations of the things we're trying to avoid dealing with on the conscious level. Dreams are an excellent way for a person to get a different perspective on their daily life. Many times we do things so often, we forget we've done them. But a dream can often shock you back into being aware of something that you do, that you were not necessarily aware of and maybe something that was antithetical to your consciously stated goals or desires in your life. When I work with patients who want to use their dreams as an augmentation to the healing process, I first of all tell them that dreams are their own symbolic language and no one else can interpret them for you. People can assist you and give you pointers and tips but it's your language and the same symbol does not mean the same thing for another person. Each dream needs to be interpreted in relation to your life and its context. If people want to work with dreams, what I sometimes do is listen to the dream and then give a possible perspective on it. Usually they will react in one of three ways. Either they'll say, "Why yes, that feels right, that feels appropriate" — in which case it's a piece of information they should take and look at more closely to find out what it has to tell them. The time in sleep is not wasted. There shouldn't be any dead spots, even when we're asleep. We still wake up the same person, so there's some element of continuity that maintains throughout sleep. The second reaction that people have is, "No, that doesn't feel right," in which case they should ignore my comments and look into the dream themselves. The third reaction is, "No, that's *definitely* not what my dream means," which means that the interpretation is probably accurate. Then the person should, in the privacy and sanctity of their own consciousness, examine the comments in relation to the dream and see what it is about the dream that upsets them so much.

We *need* to dream up until a certain point, when we're processing everything completely, when we're like a fuel that burns with no ash. When we're processing things completely in our conscious life, then I don't think we need to dream anymore. But there's a lot of work before most of us can get to that stage. A technique that might be very helpful for anyone wanting to work with their dreams is to be sure to write them down. As we start to remember, the conscious mind steps in and starts censoring. "Oops, this one; no, not this one; we'll change this a little bit, that's too obvious." And it starts censoring and changing things around so that the message of the subconscious gets diluted and distorted. It's best to write dreams down upon first remembering them. Either write them down or tape them, although I found that when I tried to tape them, it sounded so weird to hear myself speaking in the middle of the night, I didn't do it for very long. You can also give yourself conscious suggestions just before you go to sleep and re-inforce them in the hynogogic state, that twilight state just before sleep. If you re-inforce positive suggestions about remembering your dreams in a short time you'll find you *will* be remembering them. As you work with your dreams more, you'll obtain more detailed and valuable information from them.

Aging and Dying

The Eastern approach is to look at things in terms of cycles and patterns which tend to repeat in a multitude and variety of forms. The Western approach is more linear — beginning, middle, end. Things don't really end, they change. As we said before, the one thing that doesn't change is that everything changes. Things are repeated at different levels and at different times, but basic underlying patterns often remain the same. The Oriental approach is to understand that when we're born, the one thing we know for sure is that we're going to die. It's not to be accepted as, "Oh no, I have to die," but as an understanding that adds vitality to our lives and causes us to be aware of the value of being born and being alive and what a rare and unique opportunity we have. The process of aging is not viewed as, "Oh my God, we're getting closer to the thing we don't talk about that everybody's afraid of and nobody does anything about because you can't do anything about it but end up being afraid of it all the time anyway. You know?" People consequently age much more rapidly because of their fear. There are many conditions which have been labelled phobias, but essentially they connect with one fear, viewed through the kaleidoscope of individual experience. That one fear is the fear of death, the fear of not existing. Once a person deals with that then fear dissolves and one can really live. I once was working on making a film about aging and growing old and I interviewed people from India and other countries to try to show people a different perspective on the process of aging. In the United States many people get inculturated into thinking that when you hit sixty-five you have to suddenly become a senile, sexless vegetable and you get thrown out on the scrap heap. That's not true. It doesn't need to be. That's a very limiting and poor belief system that we don't need to accept. Our lives are conditioned by the belief systems we accept and when we accept limiting belief systems, we limit our experience. We limit our capacity for happiness and fullness and health and joy in our lives. Aging should be, as many people say but few believe or experience, like fine wines. They get better as they grow old. Another analogy — once you roast a coffee bean it only holds its flavor for a certain amount of time and then its flavor begins to fall off and the acid content goes up. But green beans get better as they grow older and some of the best coffee I've ever had was some thirty year old Celebes beans that had aged quite well. Aging doesn't have to have any negative connotations to it. Nor does death.

Studies have been done with people who were dying of cancer and were given LSD. The experience of LSD often involved facing their death, an issue which they had spent years avoiding. Many of the people came to the conclusion that they had never really lived and they didn't want to die. Strangely enough their cancer went into remission. Other people, upon facing death, reviewed their lives and felt that they had led good and full lives and that they were ready to die. They stopped clinging to life and within a short time, peacefully dropped their bodies. So it's how we approach it. The experience of confronting one's death, one's non-existence as an ego entity, is often the shock that causes people to reach down into their depths and experience their own true vitality that could have been experienced at any time during their lives.

Laughing, Crying and Sex

Many times when people come for treatment, they want to learn something new. Sometimes I do teach people exercises for particular problems. For example, neck and shoulders or a leg exercise or something else appropriate to their condition. When they ask further questions, I try to get them to understand that natural exercise are the best. When you have to do forced exercises, it's often because your system has not been doing the natural forms of exercise that are available.

Many people say, "What about swimming?" Swimming is great. It's a good whole body exercise. It is one, though, in which the body only moves in limited patterns because you only do certain strokes when you're in the water. But it's better than many of the other exercises that are available. The three best whole body natural exercises that I know of are: crying, laughing and sex. They all involve the whole body. When you laugh, if you really laugh, it is not only something in your mind that strikes you funny, it involves your whole body. When I was taking a yoga class, the last exercise we would do would be to lie on the floor and start to laugh, and when you're not really laughing and you're trying to laugh, it sounds so phony, it's funny. When you're in a room of twenty people who are all going, "Ha, ha, ha," it sounds so funny that you actually start laughing. When one person starts laughing, pretty soon there's a ripple of laughter throughout the room.

Laughter, like good health, is also contagious. We only think of contagion in relation to illness and disease and germs and bacteria and viruses, but it also applies to good things that can spread rapidly because there's a triggering effect in certain patterns. Laughing is a wonderful exercise for the whole body. It gets you breathing deeply, gulping air, taking it down into your lungs, giving you more oxygen, putting a sparkle in your eye, a flush on your cheeks, and a smile on your face.

Also, on the other side of the Yin-Yang balance, crying, real crying, is another whole body exercise. If you're sobbing, you often have a hard time breathing and have to gulp to take in air. It forces your body to breathe more efficiently. It involves your whole body. It gets you from your head to your toes. Laughing and crying are very similar whole body exercises that not only involve the body but the mind and the emotions in a very powerful way. Usually we're only operating with the mind or with the body and sometimes the emotions. But when you get all three going, you have an extremely powerful effect.

The other exercise that I talk to people about is sex, which if done properly, is a whole person experience. Unfortunately, for many people, it's less than a whole body experience. If the mind and the body and the emotions are involved, it too is a total experience that can revitalize and re-energize your being.

Notes

Afterword

First of all I would like to thank each and every one who bought and read the first printing of the book. The positive feedback from those initial readers has enabled me to correct minor errors that appeared in the first edition and has encouraged me to continue to communicate the information, ideas and experiences I have gathered during this life. The initial response confirmed a public interest in the principles of good health and has stimulated me to write a companion volume of mental, physical and spiritual exerciese which will provide a framework of health techniques to augment whatever belief system a person chooses to live by.

Now a few personal comments on the history of this book. When I first outlined the intent of my proposed book to my friend, patient (and patient friend) Bill Meisterfeld, he listened and when I was finished he calmly said "Well Jim, do you know what you've just done? You described a 600 page book. How about being realistic and working on something more practical and something that is more realistically accomplishable? You can always write more books you know. Don't make it so difficult that it doesn't get done. It doesn't have to be perfect the first time out. And it'll never actually become a book until you become more realistic about what you can accomplish the first time." That advice plus the persistant encouragement of Bill and his wife Charlotte and my wife, Kim, enabled me to turn experience and ideas into a book which has been a valuable learning process on many levels. I hope that what I have learned and am continuing to learn will be reflected in the quality of the subsequent books in this series. Thank you.

Additional Reading

The following list is not intended to be a comprehensive bibliography of any sort. What it does represent is a partial listing of books that are related to my perspective on health, healing, Acupuncture, Tai Chi Chuan and being-in-the-world in general. This does not mean that I agree entirely with any of them, but that I found something of value in each of them. Perhaps you will also.

Roberto Assigioli, *The Act of Will,* Penguin, 1973.

John Blofeld, *The Zen Teaching of Huang Po,* Grove Press, 1958.

Albert E. Carter, *The Miracles of Rebound Exercise,* National Institute of Reboundology & Health, 1980

George S. Clason, *The Richest Man in Babylon,* Bantam, 1981.

Don F. Draeger & Robert W. Smith, *Asian Fighting Arts,* Kodansha, 1973.

Betty Edwards, *Drawing on the Right Side of the Brain,* J. P. Tarcher, 1979.

Samuel B. Griffith (Trans.), *Sun Tzu - The Art of War,* Oxford University Press.

Napoleon Hill, *Grow Rich With Peace of Mind,* Fawcett, 1967.

Lawrence LeShan, *The Medium, the Mystic, and the Physicist,* Ballantine, 1975.

Lo/Inn/Amacker/Foe, *The Essence of T'ai Chi Ch'uan,* North Atlantic Books, 1979.

Jerry Mander, *Four Arguments for the Elimination of Television,* Morrow Quill Paperbacks, 1978.

Juan Mascaro (Trans.), *The Bhagavad Gita,* Penguin, 1962.

Miyamoto Musashi, *A Book of Five Rings,* Overlook Press, 1974.

Swami Prabhavananda & Christopher Isherwood (Trans.), *Shankara's Crest-Jewel of Discrimination,* Mentor, 1970

Oscar Ratti & Adele Westbrook, *Secrets of the Samuri,* Tuttle, 1973.

Katsuki Sekida, *Zen Training - Methods and Philosophy,* Weatherhill, 1975.

R.G.H. Siu, *Ch'i: a Neo-Taoist Approach to Life,* M.I.T., 1974.

Fred Soyka (with Alan Edmonds), *The Ion Effect,* Bantam, 1979.

Shunryu Suzuki, *Zen Mind, Beginner's Mind,* Weatherhill, 1973.

June Singer, *Androgyny - Toward a New Theory of Sexuality,* Anchor, 1977.

Karlfried Graf Von Durckheim, *Hara - The Vital Centre of Man,* Unwin Paperbakcs, 1971.

Arthur Waley (Trans.), *Monkey - Folk Novel of China by Wu Ch'eng-en,* Evergreen, 1958.